The Glorious Company

The Glorious Company

G. Avery Lee

BROADMAN PRESS
Nashville, Tennessee

© Copyright 1986 • Broadman Press
All rights reserved
4215-36
ISBN: 0-8054-1536-X
Dewey Decimal Classification: 225.92
Subject Heading: APOSTLES
Library of Congress Catalog Card Number: 86-2601

Scripture quotations are from the Revised Standard Version of the Bible, copyrighted 1946, 1952, © 1971, 1973.

Scripture quotations marked (KJV) are from the King James Version of the Bible.

Scripture quotations marked (Weymouth) are from Weymouth's *New Testament in Modern Speech* by Richard Francis Weymouth, published by special arrangement with James Clarke and Company, Ltd., and reprinted by permission of Harper and Row, Publishers, Inc.

Library of Congress Cataloging-in-Publication Data

Lee, G. Avery.
  The glorious company.

  1. Apostles—Sermons. 2. Baptists—Sermons.
3. Southern Baptist Convention—Sermons. 4. Sermons,
American. I. Title.
BS2440.L39 1986   225.9'22   86-2601
ISBN 0-8054-1536-X (pbk.)

To Bruce W. Everist, M. D.,
friend, who is in here somewhere

Preface

To be in on the beginning of almost anything is exciting. Jesus chose twelve men to be in on a beginning. After the ascension, the eleven disciples chose another believer to "fill" Judas's place. The Bible gives more information about some of the men than others. In this difficult yet exciting study of sketching the personalities of the first disciples, a lot of imagination was required. It was like taking a fingerprint and creating a personality. From the sketches in this book, we can find and see ourselves in the thirteen disciples. We have the same traits and characteristics of human nature that they had.

At first I had no plans for publishing this material. I have worked, off and on, on this study for some eight years. Over the years, some notes have been lost. I have been unable to locate the source for some of the quotations. I thought the quotations from the "Church Fathers" were in *Who's Who in the New Testament* by Donald Brownrigg. But they proved not to be. I am not a scholarly church historian but did find those references somewhere and believe they are accurate. For such negligence, I ask the reader's forgiveness.

My thanks go to my former secretary, Valerie Pierce, for typing the manuscript.

The Apostles' Creed

The most universal creed of the Christian church, the Apostles' Creed, gets its name from the tradition that it was composed phrase by phrase by the apostles. As late as the sixteenth century, the creed was printed with the name of the apostle following the phrase for which he was thought responsible. It looked like this:

I believe in God, the Father Almighty,	PETER
Maker of heaven and earth;	JOHN
and in Jesus Christ, his only Son, our Lord,	JAMES
Who was conceived by the Holy Ghost,	
born of the Virgin Mary	ANDREW
suffered under Pontius Pilate,	
was crucified, dead, and buried;	PHILIP
He descended into hell, the third	
day He rose again from the dead;	
He ascended into heaven, and	THOMAS
sitteth at the right hand of	
God, the Father Almighty;	BARTHOLOMEW
from thence He shall come to judge	
the quick and the dead.	MATTHEW
I believe in the Holy Ghost, the	
Holy Catholic Church.	JAMES, Son
	of Alphaeus
The communion of saints, the for-	SIMON, the
giveness of sin;	Zealot
the resurrection of the body;	JUDE, Son
	of James
and the life everlasting.	MATTHIAS

The Twelve Apostles as Listed in the New Testament

Matthew/Mark	Luke/Acts	John
Simon Peter	Simon Peter	Simon Peter
Andrew	Andrew	Andrew
James	James	Son of Zebedee
John	John	Son of Zebedee
Philip	Philip	Philip
Bartholomew	Bartholomew	Nathanael
Matthew	Matthew	- - -
Thomas	Thomas	Thomas
James, Son of Alphaeus	James, Son of Alphaeus	- - -
Thaddaeus	Judas, Son of James	Judas, not Iscariot
Simon, the Cananaean	Simon the Zealot	- - -
Judas Iscariot	Judas Iscariot	Judas, Son of Simon, Iscariot

Contents

1

The Glorious Company

Ephesians 4:11

Every four years, when we have a new president, one of the top news stories is the selection of the Cabinet members—those who will make up the nation's leadership. Glamour spots in the Cabinet are secretary of state and secretary of defense. Some Cabinet members get more attention than others although all are capable people. They come from divergent backgrounds, and they represent a broad spectrum of experience.

Something like that happened some two thousand years ago. A young man named Jesus, of Nazareth, was beginning a new venture. He needed men whom He could trust, who believed not only in Him but also in what He was doing. The Gospel of Mark says:

> He went up on the mountain, and called to him those whom he desired; and they came to him. And he appointed twelve, to be with him, and to be sent out to preach and have authority to cast out demons (Mark 3:13-15).

And Mark then lists the names. Luke offers a little different version:

> In these days he went out to the mountain to pray; and all night he continued in prayer to God. And when it was day, he called his disciples, and chose from them twelve, whom he named apostles (Luke 6:12-13).

Then Luke lists the names. In fact, all four Gospels give all twelve names.

Who were the twelve men Jesus called to follow Him? What do we know about them? Where do we learn about them? We don't know much about them. Three sources of information are:

1. the New Testament, although it doesn't say much;
2. traditions and legends, which are often contradictory; and
3. writings outside the New Testament, which are often based on the traditions and legends.

A fourth source is imagination, and we must make much and good use of it. Here is where we take a fingerprint and create a personality.

The twelve disciples made a diverse and sometimes rowdy group. Some men had strong personalities, and some were passive. Among the disciples were leaders and followers. There were differences of temperament: Peter, impulsive and quick to act; John, more contemplative, but with a short-tempered fuse. They differed in spiritual attitude: Nathanael, quick to believe; Thomas, slow and hesitant. There were also political differences: Matthew, a collaborator with Rome; Simon, a resister of Rome. Some were firebrands, wanting to throw a fire bomb into a crowd to get rid of those they didn't like. Some were ambitious, asking their mother to use her influence to get them the two top positions. One was a traitor to the cause. They disputed and argued among themselves. Three of them fell asleep when they should have been alert. All of the disciples deserted Jesus at the time of the greatest crisis. But eleven of them came back together.

This was not an easy group to mold into a cohesive unit. It took a person of unusual vision to see the potential for unity in such diversity. Only a man who was secure within himself, possessed of a strong self-image, and sure of his purpose could have met the challenge of molding such dissimilarity into some cohesion and, at the same time, allowing these men to keep their own distinctiveness. Jesus of Nazareth was such a person. Jesus never required total conformity, only that they believe in and follow Him. We could learn from Jesus at this point.

Who were the disciples? Eleven of them were Galileans, all from the same small area. More than half were businessmen, fishermen. The Galileans differed from the Judeans. The Judeans were more traditional and closed minded to new ideas than the Galileans. The Galileans were more spirited and independent than the Judeans. The Galileans' frustrated nationalistic hopes combined to make for speedier growth and expansion.

All twelve disciples were Jews, who must have accepted Jesus' proclaimed purpose: "I was sent only to the lost sheep of Israel" (Matt. 15:24). Twelve men were chosen as much for symbolic as practical reasons: one for each of the twelve tribes of Israel. These twelve were symbolic of the New Israel. As Moses, surrounded by the elders and the people of Israel, gave the Law on Mount Sinai, so Jesus, surrounded by the twelve and the crowds, gave the new law in a sermon on a mountain.

There is little New Testament evidence of specific activity outside of Israel by the twelve until *after* Jesus' death. Not only had they seemingly accepted Jesus' proclaimed purpose; they seemed to take Him literally when Jesus sent them out, charging them: "Go nowhere among the Gentiles, and enter no town of the Samaritans, but go rather to the lost sheep of the house of Israel" (Matt. 10:5-6). Those instructions were very spe-

cific, narrow, and limited, and almost identical to the
instructions Jesus later gave to the seventy in Luke 10:1-
11. How was Jesus' message going to win the world if He
were going to be so exclusive?

Later, after Jesus' death, Peter did have an experience
with a Roman centurion named Cornelius who believed
in Christ and was baptized (Acts 10). At that time Peter
spoke a classic sentence, "God shows no partiality."
Peter also visited the early Christian missionary head-
quarters in Antioch. But he was apparently not involved
in the later confrontation with Paul and the elders at
Jerusalem.

The only specific Christian missionaries to the Gentiles mentioned in the New Testament are Paul and his
associates. When did the original twelve begin their travels? When did Jesus' mission to Israel become universal
and extend to all people? Although it is not possible to
offer scriptural evidence of the travels of any of the
twelve, other than Peter, certain things can be inferred
from the New Testament, plus a great deal from tradition, legend, and fiction.

One tradition goes like this: High on the Mount of
Olives, below the ancient Constantinian basilica of the
Eleona, was a vast cave. In this cave, the twelve met to
divide the known world into twelve areas of mission,
each allocated to one of their number. Such a legend
goes along with the apostolic adventures to be found in
a group of five Acts of the Apostles incorporated into the
apocryphal New Testament. There, the acts of John,
Paul, Peter, Andrew, and Thomas form a rhapsody of
missionary adventure, however fanciful and undocu-
mented. Those apocryphal acts reflect the reputations of
the different members of the twelve that were circulating
in the first centuries of the Christian church. One of the

most respected works that did not find acceptance in the New Testament canon was the early second-century document called the *Didache,* or "Teaching of the Twelve."

We can see two reasons Jesus selected these men. The reasons are in Mark 3:14-16: *"to be with him, and to be sent out to preach"* (author's italics).

Any person in a leadership capacity is lonely, and the higher the place the greater the loneliness. The price of leadership is loneliness. That's why the presidency of the United States is said to be "the loneliest place in the world." Harry Truman said of the presidency: "This is a lonely job. Everybody who comes to see me wants me to do something for him. No one comes to see me for fellowship." So it was natural for Jesus to want some close associates "to be with him."

It is not too difficult to plan an ideal society, or even an ideal church, if we use our imaginations. Plato created an ideal republic; Thomas More wrote about Utopia; Bacon dreamed of a new Atlantis; and Aldous Huxley envisioned a *Brave New World.* But pen and paper cannot make the ideal real: *it takes people.* Jesus called for living people: men, not manuscripts. So far as we know, Jesus never wrote anything, except once in the sand; He wrote on/in living human lives.

These living people were then *sent out* to live and preach what Jesus had written into them and their lives. That's what the word *apostle* means. It comes from two Greek words *apo* and *stolos; stolos* meaning "sent" and *apo* meaning "away from"; thus, they were sent away from Jesus with His message.

Not one of the original twelve refused Jesus' invitation, and all but one remained steadfast. Maybe others were asked and refused; we don't know. We don't know whether these were all "first-round draft choices." I think we'd be safe in assuming that Jesus asked some who declined. Anyone who has ever sought to enlist volunteer workers has had refusals. Some of them may have been "walk ons" or "free agents." We do know that they followed Jesus when asked.

The first disciples had to meet four requirements. Those same requirements are still in effect for any twentieth-century follower of Jesus.

1. Acceptance, a profession of faith. We have to make up our minds to accept Jesus Christ as our Savior and Lord. We don't have to follow Him. No one forces us. We are asked; then we decide.

2. Self-denial, which is usually thought of in terms of giving up something. Really, it is a way of cultivating the best, most creative, and lasting qualities of life.

3. Performance. We can't just sit around; we must do something in Jesus' behalf.

4. Perseverance. We volunteer *for the duration,* no matter what comes along.

Who were the twelve men of whom John wrote from Patmos: "The wall of the city had twelve foundations, and on them the twelve names of the twelve apostles of the Lamb" (Rev. 21:14)? Well, they were people very much like us. We are going to look at them individually. We will see ourselves in one or more of them. I hope we shall learn from them and become better followers of Jesus Christ. More specifically, I trust that some new apostles-disciples shall decide to accept Jesus' invitation.

One bitterly cold day during the American Revolution while the army was wintering at Valley Forge, a small group of soldiers . . . trying to build a log hut. The soldiers' clothing was in tatters, their feet were wrapped in rags, and their hands were numbed with the cold. While they struggled to lift a heavy log in place, the officer in charge shouted orders and cursed them.

A tall, dignified man in a long dark cloak stopped to watch. He turned to the officer and said,

> "That log could easily be placed in position with the help of one more man."

> "I know that!" shouted the officer. "I've asked for more men, but headquarters won't give them to me."

> "You might give a hand yourself," suggested the gentleman.

> "Who, me? Can't you see I'm an officer? I don't do enlisted men's work."

Without a word, the tall man took off his coat, joined the men, and in a few minutes the log was in place.

> "I suppose I should thank you," sneered the officer.

> "Not necessary. I'm happy to have helped. Any time you need an extra hand, just let me know."

> "And where can I reach you, Sir?"

> "You will generally find me at headquarters. The name is Washington, Sir."

Good leaders never ask anyone to do something they will not do themselves. Example is the greatest quality of leadership. Jesus was that kind of leader. No wonder these men followed Him.

Now, what does this say to us? It says that we, too, can be a part of that glorious company, if we decide, if we will meet the requirements.

Much of the impotence of today's churches comes from the unfulfilled requirements of membership on the part of members. Our greatest danger is not from outside attack or persecution but from inside apathy and indifference. An apt description would be that some people in church resemble guests at a banquet: they can't afford to be left off the guest list, but they have been forbidden by their doctors to eat anything.

Contrast this with some delightful lines from Tennyson:

> Away with the funeral music -
> Set the pipe to powerful lips -
> The cup of Life's for him who drinks,
> And not for him who sips.

There is a startling and searching suggestiveness in a detail from French history. It was during those exciting days when Napoleon, who had escaped from the Island of Elbe, was rapidly marching toward Paris. The Bourbon monarch had fled. While waiting for Napoleon at the palace, some courtiers, preparing to turn their coats, noticed that the fleur-de-lis on the carpet of the throne room was merely sown on. Someone tugged at the lily; it came off readily. There was a bee under it: Napoleon's emblem. The next moment, ladies in court dress were hard at work tearing off the Bourbon symbols. In less than half an hour the carpet was Napoleonic once more.

Emblems of allegiance, lightly sewed on, ready to be ripped off with changing fortunes—does that describe any of us as Christians? Is our faith something we can adjust to the situation? Is our allegiance to Christ something we can change at will? Is our devotion to the church something we can remove according to the crowd? Not if we are truly disciples of Christ! Not if we have given Him the commitment of our lives!

Let's face it honestly: Church membership, being a follower of Jesus Christ, *has* lost some of its significance. The voice of the church, its preachers and members, is given little heed. Have we made discipleship, membership, too easy? Must we not call for deeper loyalty and stronger commitment from every one of us? The church is not a club where people come together out of conformity to a long-established custom on Sunday morning. The church is that glorious company called by Jesus Christ to be with Him and to be sent out with His message.

The church dare not shirk its responsibility. The church exists to proclaim the good news that in Jesus Christ there is a new way of life.

The *Te Deum* proclaims: "The glorious company of the Apostles praise thee." They set the example of true discipleship and exercise an influence on Christian faith far beyond the sum total of their individual lives. Twelve of these men are supreme examples of what God can do with the raw materials of life that are given to His use. And *we can be like them, if we will.*

2

Andrew
"Come on, I've Found Him!"
John 1:40-41

Andrew is a Greek name meaning "manly." Although his brother Peter was the skipper of the fishing boat and is given more prominence in the New Testament, Andrew was the first to be "signed on" by Jesus. He was the *protokletos*, "first to be called." And that is how the early church referred to him. We don't know what any of the apostles looked like. Early artistic portrayals of Andrew have little in common. But by the sixth century he appears as a tall man with a long head and a full beard.

The life, character, and fortunes of Andrew can be traced through three sources: (1) the Synoptic Gospels; (2) the Fourth Gospel; (3) a mass of legendary material, beginning with the third-century apocryphal writing called "The Acts of Andrew."

Four references to Andrew in the Synoptic Gospels describe Andrew's call, although Luke does not mention Andrew by name. Other references to Andrew in the Synoptics and Acts include:

—Jesus once went to the home of Peter and Andrew (Mark 1:29).
—Andrew was on the Mount of Olives, the only time he is listed with the "inner three" (Mark 13:4).
—Andrew is listed as being present in the upper room (Acts 1:13).

John's Gospel is more specific about Andrew and his functions within the group of twelve. We shall return to those episodes a bit later.

From the scriptural evidence, the character of Andrew emerges with some clarity. Although he was probably larger physically, he is always identified as "the brother of Simon Peter." Living with that kind of identification is not easy. No brother likes that. Although Andrew was the first to be called, he was not included in the "inner circle." Why didn't Jesus choose Andrew for that honor? We don't know.

One reason Andrew wasn't chosen to be part of the "inner circle" may have been Andrew's personality. Sometimes we can violate a person's personality by asking that person to do something beyond one's personal ability, or we ask people to become persons they cannot be. It is not always easy to find the right thing to ask someone to do for the true development of that person. For example, we ask someone to teach adults in Sunday School when the person would do better with children or vice versa. We ask someone to be chairperson of a committee. There is no interest in that particular committee but because of a desire to do what is asked, the person accepts the chairmanship and does a poor job. Jesus knew Andrew's abilities and probably asked him to do those tasks which matched his abilities and personality.

There is no indication that Andrew resented not being included in the inner circle. He must have thought about it, though. But whenever we see Andrew, he is doing the thing he best knew how to do—bring people to Jesus.

Compared with his bombastic brother, Andrew emerges as a sensitive and approachable man. Many large men are like that. They seem so formidable. I'm always amazed at the sensitivity of some hulking, professional football players who represent unleashed fury on the playing field but who paint, arrange flowers, play music, do needlepoint, and work with children off the field.

Andrew always had the time and patience to listen to inquiries, even from children and foreigners. He was a selfless and considerate man who did not seem to resent the leadership of his brother. That's a rare trait, for sibling rivalry can be intense and lifelong. If Andrew's brother were captain of the crew, Andrew was the "ferry man" always willing to take people to Jesus. He was a kind and faithful disciple not afraid of ridicule, even though he once offered a picnic lunch to feed a crowd. Although Jewish, he was not fearful of criticism; he enabled some Greeks to meet Jesus. Andrew has been called "the first home missionary" as well as "the first foreign missionary" of the Christian church.

Before we look more closely at Andrew in the Gospel of John, let's consider some of the legendary things that have been said about him. Remember that Eleona cave on the Mount of Olives where the twelve are said to have partitioned the world? Scythia is mentioned as Andrew's sphere of responsibility. Scythia was a wild area populated by uncivilized, ruthless barbarians. Josephus described them as "little different from wild beasts." The area would now be the southern steppes of Russia and the Ukraine, just north of the Black Sea. It is fairly certain that no Jewish colonies were there, no synagogues to form the nucleus of a Christian mission. So Andrew went as a "foreign missionary" where no one had ever been.

It's hard for us to imagine that kind of a situation today. We can read about William Carey, Adoniram Judson, and David Livingstone and get some of the picture.

We can study about some of our own early missionaries. But is there any such place in the last half of the twentieth century, someplace where Christianity has never been? The answer is yes. Here are two examples:

I have an Australian friend, Douglas Vaughan. Doug was a missionary in the "headhunter" territory of New Guinea less than twenty years ago.

I have another friend, Dr. James Young of Ruston, Louisiana. Jim was the first Christian missionary ever allowed in the country of Yemen . . . less than twenty-five years ago.

Peter's first epistle was addressed to "Pontus, Galatia, Cappadocia, Asia, and Bithynia" which border Scythia. Perhaps it is not too surprising that early legends link the mission of the two brothers in an area indicated by Peter's own writing.

A second tradition places the sphere of Andrew's ministry in Greece. The second-century anonymous apocryphal "Acts of Andrew" describe his ministry. He was persecuted, imprisoned, and executed at Patrae (Patros) about AD 60. He was said to have hung alive on a cross for two days, preaching to and encouraging those who watched him.

In AD 337 Andrew's coffin was transferred at the command of the Emperor Constantine to Byzantium, later known as Constantinople and today as Istanbul. A legend still current in Amalfi indicates that following the capture of Byzantium during the fourth Crusade in AD 1204, a certain Cardinal Capauna "took secretly" the relics of Andrew and enshrined them at Amalfi, in the Bay of Salerno. During his pontificate, Pope John XIII, in the tenth century, gave a reliquary, said to contain the face bones of Andrew, to the Greek Orthodox Church.

The final strand of legend links Andrew with Scotland.

In the seventh century, a monk named Regulus pillaged
the bones of Andrew from the relics in Constantinople.
He traveled westward and landed on the coast of Fife.
Regulus became the first bishop of Saint Andrews, and
the ruins of this magnificent church are still to be seen
in the most ancient university town in Scotland. Since
about AD 750, Andrew has been the patron saint of
Scotland. Andrew's festival is always kept in the Anglican
Church as a time of prayer for missionaries and the mission of the church.

About the same time, the remaining relics of Andrew
were transferred to Rome where, reputedly, they lie
below the great cathedral named for his brother, Peter.
Within a niche of one of the four huge piers which sup-
port the famous dome of Michelangelo is a fifteen-foot
statue of Andrew.

Now, let's go to the Fourth Gospel and see more of the
real Andrew. Three episodes were recorded by John.

The first is in John 1:35-42. Andrew and another man,
possibly Philip, seem to have been disciples of John the
Baptist. They were with John when Jesus walked by and
John said,

"Behold, the Lamb of God!"

They stayed that day with Jesus. The next morning Andrew got his brother and said,

"We have found the Messiah."

Andrew introduced Peter to Jesus. This is personal evangelism at its best. The late David T. Niles of Ceylon
described this as "one beggar telling another beggar
where he found bread."

In days past "Andrew Clubs" (groups of people dedicated to personal evangelism) were active in many cities
and towns. Today the same thing is done under the term
lay witnessing and a variety of other names.

To me, this kind of witnessing does not require a lot of training; rather, it calls for the will and desire to do it. I've never really liked the "huckster" approach to church. I like the quiet manner better, for it seems to me to be more real. Business calls this "the satisfied customer" approach. If something is meaningful to us—a good story, a good doctor, or a good purchase—we want to share it with someone else.

I don't have a brother, but I know people, some of them very well, who are not followers of Jesus. I can tell them what I have found in Jesus, what is meaningful to me about the Christian faith, and invite them to join me in it. Everyone knows someone who does not believe in Jesus.

We need to do more personal witnessing. Not witnessing because we have to but because we want to, because we believe we really have found something in Jesus Christ that is worth sharing. Some Christians are hesitant because they do not want to take advantage of a friendship or a business relationship. Some Christians go about their sharing in a positive, if very quiet, manner. And, yes, some are "anonymous Andrews."

Christians have something for which many people are searching. But, obviously, we are not sharing what we have with enough people. We are not finding our brothers and telling them what we have found. Andrew gave us a good example, if we would follow it.

The second reference to Andrew in the Gospel of John is the episode of feeding the five thousand (6:1-14). A multitude had followed Jesus. It was time to eat. Looking at the crowd, Jesus asked Philip how they could buy enough food to feed the people. Philip replied:

"Two hundred denarii would not buy enough for each of them to get a little."

At that point Andrew produced a boy with a lunch of five loaves of bread and two fish. But even Andrew's enthusiasm was dampened as he considered the incongruous scene, so he said with a shrug:

"But what are they among so many?"

The other disciples must have guffawed and kidded Andrew about that. Some people always question any proposal—especially when a lot is needed and only a little is available. Nevertheless, Andrew introduced the lad to Jesus, who took what the boy had to offer, blessed it, divided it for distribution, and fed the crowd. A lot of food was left over.

What happened? Who knows? Something miraculous took place. It always does when we share what we have. Something happens when we try. We read about how far a few dollars can go for food or medical care in some undeveloped country. No nation has been so generous in sharing what it has with other people than have the people of the United States. And no one can record the "miracles" that have taken place as those gifts have multiplied.

Andrew alone among the disciples was sensitive to the possibilities hidden within that lad and his lunch box. There were hundreds of people that day who overlooked the presence of the children in that crowd. If they were recognized at all, they were probably thought of as a nuisance. But Andrew befriended one of them. He had confidence in Jesus' ability to use what that boy had.

I know that if we were more willing to share what we have we, too, would have enough, with a lot left over. And none of us would miss out on anything.

The last appearance of Andrew is in John 12:20-22, just after what we call the triumphal entry of Jesus into Jerusalem, the last week of Jesus' earthly life. Some

Greeks came to Philip asking if they could see Jesus. Philip promptly told his friend Andrew, and together they took them to Jesus. Once again Andrew was the willing witness, introducing first his own brother, then a lad, and finally a Gentile delegation to Jesus.

Remember, Jesus had said He had come only for Israel, and He had told His disciples to go nowhere among the Gentiles or the Samaritans. It must have taken some courage for Andrew to take those Greeks to Jesus.

I know a lady who, fifty years ago, belonged to an aristocratic, affluent Baptist church in Dallas. She was a Sunday School teacher. There was a section of the city not far from that church where many Mexicans lived. In fact, it was called "Little Mexico." This was a poverty area, even by Depression standards, and long before the terms *ghetto* or *barrio* became popular. This lady started visiting and bringing Mexican children to the Gaston Avenue Baptist Church. Not all of her fellow members agreed with her or liked what she was doing. But this did not deter her; she was introducing some others to Jesus.

Years ago, in Baton Rouge, a lady named Miss Mercedes Garig gave me a book. (Her sister was Louise Garig, for whom a dormitory on the LSU campus is named.) It was a clever little book written by Gelette Burgess in 1906:

> *ARE YOU A BROMIDE*
> The Sulfitic Theory
> Expounded and Exemplified According
> to the most recent researches
> Into the Psychology of
> Boredom
> (B.W. Huebsch, New York)

The author classified people as *bromides*—flat, commonplace, tiresome, and boring—with *sulfites* as just the opposite.

The Bromide is the larger group by far. They follow the main-traveled roads; they go with the crowd. They think alike and talk alike. One may predict their opinion upon any given subject. They obey the law of averages. They are all peas in the same conventional pod. They worship dogma. Bromides conform to everything sanctioned by the majority and may be depended upon to be trite, banal, and arbitrary. The Bromides have no surprises for you. They may be wise and good, loved and respected, but they live inland; they never put out to sea. They are always there when needed, always the same.

Who then are the Sulfites? They are persons who do their own thinking, those who have a few surprises up their sleeves. They are explosive. One can never foresee what they will do, except that it will be a spontaneous manifestation of their own personalities. Sulfites come together like mercury in this bromidic world. The Bromides we have always with us. The Sulfites appear uncalled. This does not mean they are always agreeable company. By their nature, they must continually surprise us with the unexpected. You never know what they will say or do. They will not bore us, and they may well shock us.

Which are we, you and I? Perhaps some of each. I think our man Andrew had some combination of both. Maybe another word we could use, a somewhat milder word than *sulfite*, would be *catalyst*—something that makes something happen, that brings about change. I think Andrew was a mild catalyst. He did things that brought about change. He made things happen.

3

Peter

"Act Now, Think Later"
Luke 5:8; Matthew 14:28

The theme of Peter's life could be summarized in two of his own statements:

"Depart from me, for I am a sinful man, O Lord" (Luke 5:8).
Lord, if it is you, bid me come to you" (Matt. 14:28).

Peter seemed always to be in the process of going toward Jesus, going away, and then coming back again. The course of Peter's life portrays a man's journey from shifting small stones, *petra,* to solid rock, *petros,* and all that is in between: sometimes slippery, sometimes steadfast. Historians refer to Peter as impulsive, impetuous, and irresponsible. Others speak of him as the one who denied even knowing Jesus. To the disciples, Peter was their spokesman. To Jesus, he was "the Rock." Novelist Lloyd Douglas called him *The Big Fisherman.* Taken singly, none of these expressions is adequate; taken together, they still do not tell us everything about the man.

Of all the personalities of the apostles, we know more about Peter than any other. We are attracted to Peter because he is so human, because of his constant mistakes and subsequent restoration, because of his boisterous and impetuous enthusiasm, and for his always-good intentions. Peter was the natural leader, not only of the original twelve but of all the disciples. And although his

31

leadership of the early church, especially during the expansion of the church, seems to have been superceded by Paul, nevertheless, Peter became the traditional first bishop of Rome.

In the four Gospels, other than the name of Jesus, no name is mentioned more often than Peter: 96 times. Peter's name appears 58 times in the Acts and 7 other places in the New Testament for a total of 161 times. Only Paul is named more often in the New Testament, 184 times, but 29 of those are in Paul's own writings.

No disciple spoke more often. Jesus spoke more often to Peter than to any other apostle. No other disciple so boldly confessed and outspokenly encouraged Jesus as Peter repeatedly did. And no one intruded, interfered, and bothered Him as repeatedly as Peter did. Jesus spoke words of approval, praise, and even blessing to Peter, the like of which He never said to anyone else. On the other hand, and in almost the same breath, Jesus said harsher things to Peter than to any of the other twelve.

Peter's name always heads the list of the twelve apostles, although he was not the first to be called. There is a sense in which the twelve could be called "the brothers of Bethsaida," for *beth saida* means "fisher village." There were many such villages, perhaps ten, around the north shore of the Sea of Galilee. All but one of the twelve, Judas Iscariot, were Galileans, and more than half of them were professional fishermen.

Here's the scene. Jesus had been teaching the people from Simon's boat. When He stopped speaking, He told Simon to cast his nets on the other side of the boat. The catch was so large that "they beckoned their partners in the other boat to come and help them." Then Peter fell to his knees and said,

"Depart from me, for I am a sinful man, O Lord."

Jesus responded,
"Do not be afraid: henceforth you will be catching men."
The fishermen left their nets to follow Jesus (Luke 5:1-11).

Though Peter was usually the spokesman for the twelve, talk did not satisfy him. He had to be doing something. Peter's personality was "act now, think later." This can be seen in four episodes.

(1) Caught up in the emotional exhilaration of the mount of transfiguration, Peter blurted out, "Let's build three tabernacles and stay here forever." That often happens to us. We want to maintain our high emotional experiences. But we can't. Jesus and the three had to go down to the valley where people lived, where human needs must be met. The mountaintop experiences are to prepare us for the everyday affairs.

(2) Seeing Jesus walk on the water, Peter got out of the boat and started toward Him, not thinking about what He was doing. Then Peter's faith faltered, and he began to sink. But he had started! The others sat in the boat.

(3) In the garden of Gethsemane, Peter drew his sword and cut off a guard's ear. How did he get out of that alive?

(4) Later, that same night, Peter denied even knowing Jesus.

In all this, we see Peter as an uninhibited person who spoke and acted impulsively, guided by feeling more than thought. He was capable of great heights of exaltation, and he was also subject to great depths of despair.

There were four major turning points in Peter's life.

First, that time when Peter said:
"You are the Christ, the Son of the living God" (Matt. 16:16).

And Jesus answered:

"You are Peter, and on this rock I will build my church" (Matt. 16:18).

Another major turning point was when Peter denied even knowing Jesus (Matt. 26:69-75). When Jesus predicted the denial, Peter adamantly rejected such nonsense. Everyone else might deny, but not Peter! Even in Gethsemane, when the soldiers came, Peter valiantly drew his sword, went to Jesus' defense, and cut off a soldier's ear. That was dangerous and foolhardy. That Peter got out of that alive is amazing. At least we cannot doubt Peter's physical courage. But moral courage is something else and far more difficult.

After the melee, Peter found himself in a courtyard. How can we imagine his feelings? There is an exquisite descriptive phrase in Mark's account: "One of the maids of the high priest came; and seeing Peter warming himself" (Mark 14:66). There he was: distraught, discouraged, and despondent, sitting around a fire in the loneliness of desolation and defeat; Peter's dreams were crushed, and this young woman said:

"You also were with the Nazarene."

Peter denied it. Another identified him (How could anyone not recognize him?), and again Peter denied. Then a bystander said:

"Certainly you are one of them; you are a Galilean, your accent betrays you."

And Peter began to curse, salty-fisherman curses,

"I do not know this man!"

At that moment, a rooster crowed. Luke adds another memorable phrase,

"The Lord turned and looked at Peter."

And Peter went out and wept bitterly.

Isn't this an experience we have all had: losing our

confidence in a tense situation, scared, wanting to save our own hides—we denied our faith, denied any knowledge of Jesus? Maybe our experience wasn't so dramatic, but it was just as real. But that look of Jesus, a loving, understanding, forgiving look, caused repentance and restored our confidence, and we were ready to try again.

The third turning point was after the resurrection (John 21:16). Even with a bit of restored confidence, Peter was not altogether sure. He did what we would have done: Peter turned back to the familiar to get his bearings. He went fishing, and six other apostles went with him. The fishing was bad. At daybreak they saw a stranger on the shore who told them to try the other side of the boat, which they should have had sense enough to do anyway. They did and got a big catch. Finally, perhaps, the early morning mist cleared. Recognizing Jesus, Peter sprang into the sea and splashed to the shore, where Jesus already had a fire going. After breakfast, Jesus had a little talk with Peter. Remember the old Stamps-Baxter song: "Just a little talk with Jesus makes it right"? Three times Jesus asked Peter if he loved Him, getting an affirmative answer each time, and each time telling Peter to "feed" His sheep.

Scholars tell us that the first two times Jesus used a word for love which meant an unconditional commitment. But Peter responded with a word that had some reservations. Finally, Jesus switched to Peter's word, as if to say:

"Very well, I'll take what you give and use that."

Not many of us are ready or willing for the all-out giving of ourselves to Jesus Christ. We want to hold back a little, no matter how strongly we believe in and love Him. As the old saying goes: "The world has yet to see what can happen when persons give themselves wholly to Christ." Well, some have come close. It is encouraging to the rest of us to see what can be done even with our limited, reserved giving of ourselves.

The fourth turning point was when Peter preached to Cornelius, the Roman centurion, and Cornelius was converted (Acts 10:36-43). Not only was this occasion a unique event in the extension of Christian faith in the non-Jewish world, but the sermon represents a superb summary of the Christian gospel. I doubt if we can grasp the dramatic trauma Peter faced. Was this "Way" to be an exclusive continuation to "the house of Israel," or was it to become inclusive so as to include Gentiles? Was he a devout Jew with no love for Gentiles, especially Roman soldiers, to offer one of them God's way of salvation? Then Peter had that remarkable insight:

"Truly I perceive that God shows no partiality, but in every nation anyone who fears him and does what is right is acceptable to him."

This lesson of inclusiveness, that God shows no partiality or "God is no respecter of persons" as the King James Version puts it, is such a hard thing that 2,000 years later we have not fully learned it. Nor are we always willing to practice it without reservation.

Peter's experience with Cornelius and Paul's influence helped Peter liberalize his strict Judaism. At the Jerusalem conference, these two established Christian leaders agreed that Gentile converts could join the Christian Way without the Jewish ceremonial circumcision. However, under pressure from the strict Judaistic group in Jerusalem, notably James, Peter later reversed himself. The narrow legalisms had a strong hold on Peter. He began to withdraw fellowship from the uncircumcized Gentiles.

At that point, Paul rebuked Peter for such a backward step:

"When Cephas [Peter] came to Antioch I opposed him to his face" (Gal. 2:11).

Peter's fluctuating positions caused a lot of confusion in the community of faith. Small wonder that the early church fathers called him *Petra,* meaning "little stones." Small, smooth, shifting pebbles are not a good foundation on which to build a house, much less a church or a life or a religious faith. Yet the name was quite appropriate for a man of Peter's changeable nature.

But no matter how often Peter wavered or failed, he would get up and try again. He was the true and undoubted leader of the church, facing with inspiring courage and humility the consequent persecution and punishment.

We know little of Peter's work outside Palestine. We do know he visited Antioch. He seems to have visited Corinth (1 Cor. 1:12). He may have been engaged in evangelism in Rome before Paul got there. Certainly, Eusebius and Origin declare that Peter went to Rome. Since AD 160 there has been a memorial over a grave reputed to be that of Peter. So let's close our look at Peter by seeing him in Rome.

Tradition says that Peter did go to Rome. Although there is no New Testament evidence, it is reasonable to assume that he did. "All roads lead to Rome," it was said, and everyone wanted to go there. There was a great tidal wave of persecution in Rome. Some of the Roman Christians persuaded Peter that the greater good would be for him to escape so that he could continue his work. Peter would be more valuable alive to them than dead. So he left. As he was leaving the city, Peter had a vision of Jesus entering the city. When he saw Jesus, Peter asked:

"*Quo vadis?* [Where are you going?]"

"I am coming to Rome to be crucified."

"Lord, are you being crucified again?"

"Yes, Peter, I am being crucified again."

Even at the end, in that *Quo Vadis* legend, Peter wavered. But the people had persuaded him against his will. Whereupon Peter turned around and went back into the city of Rome. He was no longer Simon *Petra,* little stones; he was Simon *Petros,* solid rock! Peter had made his last change of position. He was the "Rock" Jesus said he would become. Peter was crucified, just as his Master was. But feeling unworthy, he said so, just as he had on earlier occasions. Legend has Peter asking to be crucified head downward.

"Depart from me, for I am a sinful man, O Lord."

"Lord, if it is you, bid me come to you."

"So Peter got out of the boat . . . and came to Jesus."

4

James
"A Capacity for Anger"
Mark 1:15-21; Luke 9:51-55

With ten large townships encircling the Sea of Galilee and the additional ten townships called the Decapolis, there was a vast demand for fresh fish. Consequently, there was a thriving fishing industry in that region. Great quantities of fish were needed at the great feasts by the multitudes of faithful pilgrims coming to the Temple in Jerusalem. Fish was pickled or dried at Capernaum and other centers, then packed in barrels and transported by camels and donkeys to Jerusalem and Samaria. The larger fishing concerns would have their own offices, sales and marketing representatives, and distribution warehouses in Jerusalem and elsewhere. It is not too far-fetched for us to say that Jonah and Sons, Andrew and Peter, were in partnership with Zebedee and Sons, James and John.

Those fishermen disciples of Jesus were far from being poor, simple, ignorant, rustic peasants. I think we've overdrawn that picture of them. They were astute businessmen in a big, competitive industry. Zebedee and his family were of financial substance and social status with considerable skill and business acumen. Zebedee employed a hired crew and had at least one ship large enough for deep-sea fishing. It is not unlikely that these two families were thus linked in a partnership involving the packing, transport, and distribution of the fish they caught. That's big business!

James and John had a close familial link with both John the Baptist and Jesus. Their mother and Jesus' mother were sisters, daughters of Joachim and Anna. That made them first cousins of Jesus, and relatives of John the Baptist, who was Jesus' cousin. They all probably knew each other.

The call of the sons of Zebedee seems to have happened at the same time and place as that of Andrew and Peter:

> And going on a little farther, he saw James the son of Zebedee and John his brother, who were in their boats mending the nets. And immediately he called them; and they left their father Zebedee in the boat with the hired servants, and followed him (Mark 1:19-21).

Jesus nicknamed the two brothers "Boanerges" (3:17), an Aramaic term meaning "sons of thunder." This could have been a reference to Zebedee himself as a "terrible-tempered Mr. Bang." Maybe he was a hard-nosed businessman who asked no quarter and gave none in the rough and tumble fishing business, where rough men gained respect by toughness. More generally we have implied that the term is for the brothers, presumably referring to their own temperaments. If so, did the nickname come in a humorous, good-natured chiding, or was it a rebuke? I think it was probably more the good-natured kidding. But there were times when Jesus did come down hard on them. The characters of both James and John that emerge from the first three Gospels is that they were men of considerable ambition, explosive temper, and at times intolerant.

Despite their temperaments and Jesus' frank reprimands, these two brothers, James and John, along with Peter, formed an inner circle within the group of apostles. Jesus took those three along on at least three occasions. Yes, I guess we can say that this was a sort of favoritism on the part of Him who played no favorites and even reproved them for asking for the top places. But any group needs a kind of "executive council."

James, the son of Zebedee, was born and reared along the beautiful shores of Galilee, and Galilee is beautiful. As a boy, he swam in its clear, azure waters, learning as he went along. He knew the capricious nature of that sea. As a man, James joined his father and brother in the family fishing business. It is reasonable to assume that James was a successful businessman, that he was respected in the community, and that he was congenial in his personal relationships, despite his temper. He was well above the average in intelligence, talent, ability, and capacity for work. Maybe we could call James one of "the good ol' boys" of Capernaum.

And, yes, he was ambitious. There's nothing wrong with that. Who'd give a Palestinian fig for a man who was not ambitious! One time James and John wanted the right- and left-hand positions in Jesus' coming Kingdom. There are two versions of this episode. In Mark 10:35-40, the brothers themselves ask; in Matthew 20:21-23, their mother asks for them. Many a mother has been overly ambitious for her children. Every parent ought to be, and we are. After all, she was Jesus' aunt! Naturally, the other ten were indignant and said so. Jesus let all the disciples know that they didn't know what they were asking and had no right to ask. Anyway, those places were not his to give; they had to be earned: "Whoever would be great among you must be your servant, and

whoever would be first among you must be slave of all"
(Mark 10:43-44).

By nature, James was intense and hotheaded. His
short-fused quick temper is seen in an episode recorded
in Luke 9:51-55. En route to Jerusalem the group
stopped in a Samaritan village. Because the Samaritans
were prejudiced against Jews, the Samaritans refused the
disciples hospitality, and that was a breach of Middle
East ethics and custom. James turned white-hot with anger. He wanted to call down fire from heaven and destroy all of them.

"Who do they think they are, these half-breed Samaritans, to deny hospitality to the Messiah!"

I've never had such an experience of rejection. You
probably haven't either. But it has happened to people
whom we know: Irish, Catholics, Italians, Orientals, and
some Protestants. Perhaps the most notable rejections
have been directed toward Jews and Blacks.

Jesus calmed James down by saying:

"James, you ol' hotheaded Boanarges, I can understand your feelings, but you don't understand what
I've been saying. I didn't come to destroy anyone or
anything, but I came to save. You must love your
neighbor as you love yourself; that's part of this new
way I'm telling you about."

Then, somewhere along the way, Jesus told the story of
the good Samaritan (see Luke 10:30-37).

Such experiences led James to see that the spirit of
violence and revenge is contrary to the spirit of Christ.
He learned, as Elijah had before him, that the fire from
heaven and the sword of human hate will never bring
God's kingdom. The kingdom of love and service comes
in a different way.

There are only two recorded statements from James:

the one where he asked for the top position and his wanting to call down fire on the Samaritans. What if, many years from now, all people would know about us were two things we had once said in a thoughtless time of anger or in a careless time of self-seeking? What if we could have time to think and formulate a sentence which we believe would better describe us and reflect our true selves? What two sentences would we want to leave behind? My two would be:

In the constant tension between the ideal and the actual, things as they ought to be and as they are, the ought and the is, we try step by achievable step to bring the two closer together.

So long as persons feel that they are
    loved by God,
    loved at home,
    and have a sense of purpose in what
    they are doing,
they can take anything life throws their way.

James was one of the three who formed an inner circle within the apostles. On three occasions only these disciples went with Jesus:

1. The healing of Jairus's daughter (Luke 8:49-51).
2. The mount of transfiguration (Matt. 17:1-2).
3. The garden of Gethsemane (Mark 14:32-33).

So let's take a brief look at those occasions. We learn nothing about James other than that he was present. Something of what happened must have rubbed off on James so as to influence him in later years.

In the Jairus case, James saw that someone cared about people: Jairus cared about his daughter, and Jesus cared about both. In that world, as well as in our own, it is easy to overlook such caring. We tend to get so wrapped up in our own affairs that we forget that other people have problems too. Sometimes we are negligent, and sometimes we just procrastinate about doing what we want to do.

Try as I may—and I don't always try hard enough—I don't do all that I can to let other people know that someone cares for them. Sometimes I don't know who needs caring for. Sometimes my own concerns weigh so heavily that I forget about others. Sometimes I procrastinate. And sometimes I do get the feeling across to someone else that I do care. Sometimes, no matter what one does it is not enough; some people just don't get the message or they always want a little bit more.

A traveler tells how she was traveling in Soviet Georgia in the days before the second world war. She was taken to see a very humble, poor, old woman in a little cottage. The old peasant woman asked the traveler if she were going to Moscow. Learning that she was, the old woman asked:

"Then, would you mind delivering a parcel of homemade toffee to my son?"

The son's name was Joseph Stalin. He couldn't get toffee in Moscow.

We do not normally think of the late brutal dictator of all Russia as a man who liked toffee, but his mother did! She loved him and cared for him. No matter what our condition or how evil we may be, someone loves us. Most of all, God loves us. That's the reason Jesus came, to tell us and to show us that God loves and cares for us. James learned that in Jairus's home.

Without elaboration, what may have rubbed off on James on the other two occasions? On the mount of transfiguration, James was reminded of the transcendent glory of God, the approval of God on Jesus, and Jesus' connection with God's purpose. James was a part of something eternal, not a fly-by-night transient ministry. In Gethsemane James learned what it is to be fully committed to the will of God, even if he didn't hear all of Jesus' agonizing prayer because he was asleep. James did get the impetus for his own continuation in the adventure he had joined at Galilee.

About fifteen years after that call by the lakeside, James became the political victim of King Herod Agrippa I, being executed shortly before Agrippa's own death. The account is in Acts 12:1-3:

> About that time Herod the king laid violent hands upon some who belonged to the church. He killed James the brother of John with the sword; and when he saw that it pleased the Jews, he proceeded to arrest Peter also.

James's martyrdom, described in a single sentence of seven Greek words, is the only reliable and the only biblical record of the death of any of the original apostles other than Judas Iscariot's suicide. The chances are that such a report would not have been recorded unless James was an outstanding person.

There is no further scriptural reference to James, son of Zebedee. Outside the New Testament, James is scarcely mentioned.

Tradition links James with Spain. Throughout medieval Christendom until the sixteenth century, believers accepted that James had preached Christianity in Spain. After that, better scholarship began to question that tradition.

The legend goes that during James's mission in Spain, Mary, the mother of Jesus, while still living, was miraculously transported from Palestine to Spain. Accompanied by angels bearing a marble pillar, she came to the banks of the river Ebro. She talked with James and told him to build a church dedicated to her on the site where the pillar had been placed. The site is now the basilica of the church of *Nuestra Senora del Pillar* at Saragosa. The legend continues that after James's execution in Jerusalem, the apostle's body was taken to Galicia in northwest Spain and buried at a place where now stands the *Cathedral of Santiago de Compostela,*, Saint James of the Field of Stars. In the ninth century, according to the legend, James appeared on earth and helped the Spanish army win a decisive victory over the Moors. The Santiago creed remains an active element in Spanish life today.

Although James is the patron saint of Spain, and *Iago* is a popular Spanish name, any actual historical connection between James and Spain in the brief decade or so between Pentecost and his execution by Herod Agrippa is unlikely. However, Paul did refer to Spain in Romans 15:23 as if some Christians were there. There was time enough and the means of transportation for James to have gone to Spain, stayed awhile, and then to have returned to Jerusalem. Maybe James did get to Spain. Who knows?

Eusebius relates an experience which supposedly took place at James's trial before Herod Agrippa. In James's last hour, the peace and love evident in his face and in his words convicted his accuser. Deeply moved, Josias fell down before James as he was being led away for execution and begged forgiveness, declaring his own acceptance of Christian faith. James lifted Josias to his feet, placed on his forehead the kiss of forgiveness, and said, "Peace be with you."

It is unfortunate that although James was one of the inner circle, there is so little factual information about him. His was the shortest ministry, and his brother's was perhaps the longest of any of the twelve.

A Roman coin engraved with two oxen, one facing an altar and the other a plow, illustrates the respective destinies of "the sons of thunder." The coin bears the inscription "Ready for Either," the brief moment of sacrifice or the long furrow.

James had learned how to keep his ambition in perspective, how to keep his temper under control, and his intolerance had given way to acceptance of those who differed with him. He had learned what Jesus had said:
  Whoever of you who would be great, or wants to be
  first, must learn to be a servant of everyone.
James had earned his place in Jesus' company of love and service.

5

John
"Lovable Son of Thunder"
John 3:16-21

As a boy, following the fishing business, John must have been accustomed to hard work and danger. Exposed to all kinds of weather and to all the risks associated with the sea, John's manliness must have developed so as to stand him in good stead in his later years of exile. Because of his father's profitable business, John never knew poverty and hardship until he shared it with Jesus, even if then. Some children born in the lap of luxury with silver spoons in their mouths are able to become strong and self-reliant.

John was strong and daring, with courage equal to any emergency, and never frightened by ordinary fear. He and James had the same ambitious drive to excel and the same explosive temper. But John was also tender. Can it be that John's tough mind and tender heart caused Jesus to trust him so much?

Perhaps John's temperament suited his place in the household and he was allowed more indulgence than his older brother. John may have been his father's favorite, "the child of blessing," as Myron Madden would say. Maybe he was a bit on the spoiled side and expected "first place" in everything from everyone. We might say that he was the gifted son, the genius of the family. He was endowed with the insight of the poet and the foresight of the prophet. These are spiritual qualities, qualities which prompted him to respond to the wave of excitement created by John the Baptist. This in turn caused him to sign on with Jesus as the wave of the future.

Being tough-minded, tenderhearted, family favorite, and considerate of others is an unusual combination, but John seems to be that combination. Not that he was perfect, far from that. We see him angry. We see him ambitious. We see him staking out the claim as being "the disciple whom Jesus loved." But as the English philosopher John Locke put it: "God, when he makes a prophet, does not unmake the man." John, lovable son of thunder, was altogether human.

Tradition says that John was a mystic: quiet, reserved, timid, and gentle. Artists have pictured him as a saint with a halo around his head, soft hands, and a feminine face. That is *not* the New Testament picture of John. The real John of the New Testament was a different kind of man. Although he was the youngest of the twelve, he was a fisherman, deeply tanned, with skin toughened by constant exposure to the wind and sun, strong shoulders and tough hands made rugged and sturdy from pulling on boat oars and fishing nets. He was occasionally given to strong outbursts of emotion, probably accompanied by an earthy vocabulary. Sensitive, mystical poet, yes, but as strong and rugged as the prophet Amos or the man from the wilderness, John the Baptist.

One day John stood on the edge of a crowd gathered around a man possessed of demons (Mark 9:38-40). Someone was saying,

"In the name of Jesus of Nazareth, come out from him."

Hearing the name of the Lord, John naturally moved closer. As the crowd dispersed, he asked the man doing

the exorcising of the demon if he were one of Jesus'
disciples. When the man said he was not, John com-
manded the man to stop. Obviously pleased with himself, John reported to Jesus what he had done:

"Teacher, we saw a man casting out demons in your
name, and we forbade him, because he was not following us."

But instead of receiving Jesus' approval, John got a
sound put-down:

"Don't stop him . . . he who is not against us is for us."
John was so blindly attached to his own particular group
that he could not see any good in the work of those who
belonged to a variant group.

He was like the narrow-minded preacher who had
been helping clergyman of another faith with a community project. When the job was done, the second said to
the first:

"After all, our differences are much less important
than our agreements. We are both working for the
same great end."

"Yes," replied the other, "we are both doing the
Lord's work—you in your way, and I in His."

We could take a lesson here, for we sometimes act as
if we are God's only children. Taking a leaf from John's
book, we refer to ourselves as

"Those Christians whom God loves."

Well, God does love us, but He loves us all: equally. I am
a Baptist, and prefer being one to any other Christian
group I know. But I believe the day is fast approaching
when we must all come closer together, for the forces
against us are gathering strength. It is time for us to say:

"Who serves my Father as a son or daughter is surely
kin to me."

John was so intensely devoted to his own religious

persuasion and to the work of the twelve that he was unaware of the fact that there might be other forms of belief or other credible avenues of service. From Jesus he learned how wrong it is to label as false the faith of another because it is different from one's own. John's horizons were enlarged; his vision was broadened. He lost his air of superiority and overcame his feeling of advantage. After Jesus' resurrection, John placed his hands on the heads of new Samaritan converts, preached to the Gentiles, preserved the prayer of Jesus "that they may be one, even as we are one" (John 17:11), and put his stamp of approval on the ministry of Paul.

There is little more information in the Synoptic Gospels about John than about his brother James. There are two references made about John in the last day or so before the crucifixion, Mark 13:3-4 and Luke 22:8, when Jesus sent him and Peter to prepare for the Passover.

In the Gospel of John, we get more insight into the kind of apostle John was. That Gospel is called "the gospel of conversations." Twenty-four of Jesus' conversations with seventeen different people are recorded in John. Almost half of the words are the words of Jesus. John's statement as to the purpose and content of his writing is given toward the end of his Gospel: "These are written that you might believe that Jesus is the Christ, the Son of God, and that believing you might have life in his name" (20:31).

From John's stated purpose, we can see that he wanted other people to know and love Jesus as he did. He loved Jesus and felt especially loved by Jesus. The term *the disciple Jesus loved* is used only by the writer of the Fourth Gospel, and he used it on four occasions:

(1) In the upper room: The disciple "whom Jesus

loved" was reclining next to Jesus at the Supper" (13:23).

(2) At Calvary: "Jesus saw his mother, and the disciple whom he loved standing near" (19:26).

(3) On resurrection morning when Mary Magdalene found the tomb empty and the stone rolled away," she ran, and went to Simon Peter and the other disciple, the one whom Jesus loved" (20:2).

(4) Later, at Galilee, after the fruitless night of fishing, a stranger is seen on the shore. "That disciple whom Jesus loved said to Peter, 'It is the Lord!' " Following Jesus' "Feed my sheep" conversation with Peter, Peter turned "and saw following them the disciple whom Jesus loved, who had lain close to his breast at the supper" (21:7-20).

I suppose we can forgive this bit of self-indulgence on John's part. Having been the "family favorite" and knowing that Jesus was very fond of him, it was perhaps natural for John to feel that he was Jesus' favorite, also.

There are legends aplenty about John's later life, including one where he went to Rome and survived being thrown into a cauldron of boiling oil and being forced to drink a cup of hemlock poison! The most likely circumstance is that he was exiled to Patmos under a decree from the Emperor Domitian. Those orders were later revoked, and those who had been exiled were restored. When John left Patmos, he went to Ephesus, where he became a sort of bishop and lived to an old age. One story from Jerome in the year 300 puts it this way:

> When John tarried in Ephesus to extreme old age, and could only with difficulty be carried to the church in the arms of his disciples, and was unable to give utterance to many words, he used to say no more at their several meetings than this: "Little

children, love one another." At length the disciples and fathers
who were there, wearied with always hearing the same words,
said: "Master, why dost thou always say this?" "It is the Lord's
command," was his reply, "and, if this alone be done, it is
enough."

In the Fourth Gospel and epistles, John gave to the
world a definition of love not to be found in the writings
of any other author, religious or secular. He had learned
the lesson of love from close personal contact with Jesus
Himself. John knew that the love of Jesus held him cap-
tive. He resolved the gospel as a theory of life as well as
a practical experience into the one principle of love.

Some eighty times, John used the term in his writings.
To him, the love of which Jesus spoke was not a senti-
ment but a principle, a life-changing principle. To him,
love was life and the test of love was in keeping Jesus'
commandments. Let's see a nine-point classification of
John's concept of divine love.

1. God is a God of love: 5:42; 15:10.
2. God loved His Son: 10:17; 15:9; 17:23-26.
3. God loved the disciples: 16:27; 17:23.
4. God loves the world, all people: 3:16.
5. God is loved by Christ: 14:31.
6. Christ loved the disciples: 13:1-34.
7. Christ loved individuals: 11:5,36; 13:23.
8. Christ expected all people to love Him and God:
   8:42; 14:23.
9. Christ taught that we should love one another: 13:
   34-35; 15:12-13.

I think two passages summarize this for us: One is in
the Gospel (13:34-35); the other is in the First Epistle
(3:14):

A new commandment I give to you, that you love one another;

even as I have loved you, that you also love one another. By this all men will know that you are my disciples, if you have love for one another.

We know that we have passed out of death into life, because we love the brethren.

The early Christians practiced that, even in their disputes. That's one reason they had a changing effect on their society. Said one of their critics: "See how those Christians love one another."

There is another version of Jerome's story about the aged John. The highly respected John was invited to preach in the church at Ephesus. His coming was widely publicized. On the appointed day a vast multitude assembled, filling every available place in the church and the area around it.

When John arrived, he was so feeble that he had to be carried into the church. After eloquent words of welcome and a lengthy preparatory service, such as prominent people are subjected to, John was lifted to his feet to speak. A great hush came over the congregation. Everyone strained to hear. The aged man said:

"Little children, love one another, love one another, love one another."

He sat down, his sermon over. Many went home disappointed. They shook their heads and said:

"It is too bad that the old man is in his dotage. Why doesn't he stop trying to preach?"

But others realized that simple and brief sermon of the old man, such as it was, contained the heart of the gospel. It is the insight of the saint, not the infirmity of the senile, that says:

"Little children, love one another!"

6

Philip

"Take Advantage of the Situation"
John 14:8-11

In reading the Bible, one is impressed that the forty or so writers of the sixty-six books were both annalists and analysts of high order and competence. They were word-space economists long before book and article digests or capsule summaries of the news came on the scene. They were not given to recording unimportant details, though sometimes the trivia they did record has amazing insight. At times we do feel that the biographical data is scanty and we wish for more. Yet we can distinguish features and characteristics if we read between the lines, use our imagination, and bring alongside other knowledge we may find.

The writers of the Synoptic Gospels were annalists—that is, they recorded the external facts of the life of Jesus Christ. But the writer of the Fourth Gospel used the historical data to unfold the drama of Jesus at work with people. We see this principle at work in the apostle named Philip. All the Synoptics say about Philip is to include his name in the list of the twelve chosen by Jesus. John was the only writer to tell anything about the man, something about his individuality. John was an analyst. And even John gave us precious little, only recording four events which involved Philip: 1:43-48; 6:5-7; 12:20-23; and 14:8-9.

Philip is always mentioned fifth in the listings of the apostles. In each list he is the first to be mentioned after Peter, Andrew, James, and John. Philip's home was in Bethsaida in northern Galilee. Like Andrew, his name was Greek, though we have every reason to believe that he was a devout Jew. In Greek, the name *Philip* means "lover of horses." This has given rise to the tradition that he might have been an expert horseman and a charioteer among the Romans who occupied the garrisons of his community. Being from Bethsaida, he is more likely to have been a fisherman. But why not both? Businessmen do have outside avocations.

Philip was first found in Judea on the day after Jesus' baptism. Probably Philip was among those from Galilee who had gone to Judea to hear John the Baptist. He and his friend Nathanael were watching and waiting for the long-expected Messiah. There is no record of the details, only that Jesus said to Philip,

"Follow me."

and Philip accepted the invitation. From that brief encounter, Philip went to tell Nathanael that he had found the one whom they expected:

"We have found him of whom Moses in the law and also the prophets wrote, Jesus of Nazareth, the son of Joseph" (1:42-45).

The names of Philip and Nathanael (Bartholomew) are inseparably linked in the Synoptics which do no more than list their names. However, the Fourth Gospel describes a number of incidents involving them both, and some estimate of their characters and personalities may be deduced.

There were two Philips in the early church. One is specified as "the apostle"; the other is variously called the "deacon" or "evangelist." These references are in

Acts. From the second century, many scholars have identified the two as the same man. Polycarp, Papias, and Eusebius all identified them as being the same person. This seems illogical since the deacons were selected and set aside by the disciples or the early church. However, it could have happened; Some churches have ordained clergymen who have been asked to serve as deacons. I am inclined to believe these were two different men and for our purposes shall not include anything about Philip the deacon-evangelist.

Philip seems to have been a sincere person, practical and approachable, but more of a "contact" man than a leader. While not the most scintillating of the apostles, Philip was chosen; so he must have had some kind of ability. "The matter-of-fact man" is what Dean Brown of Yale called him. Despite Philip's limitations, Jesus put a value on him. Jesus saw Philip as a man of worth. He sensed something that would make Philip useful. You see, Jesus can use any kind of personality and ability. In Jesus' eyes no one is unimportant or insignificant.

At the outset, we see Philip as a man of inquiring mind. In his testimony to Nathanael, "We have found him," Philip showed that he had studied the Scriptures and knew about the Messiah. So Philip, matter-of-factly, accepted and followed because he believed that Jesus met the Old Testament requirements. Even so, Philip was slow to grasp the full significance. But aren't we all? He may have made a quick decision, but his perception of the meaning of what he had done was slow—just like many of us.

We see Philip cooly rationalistic and practical in the episode of the feeding of the five thousand. The enthusiasm of the crowd did not cause Philip to lose sight

of the financial facts. When Jesus suggested buying
bread to feed the crowd, Philip was staggered:

"Why, two hundred denarii would not buy enough for
each to get a little."

He knew too much arithmetic to be adventurous. I don't
think this was due to any lack of faith on Philip's part; it
was just common sense.

To suggest that Philip had a matter-of-fact side en-
dears him to many. Some of the others seem so formidable that when we see one like Philip we take heart for
ourselves. To think of him as dull and lacking in faith is
to misrepresent him. If Philip were a bit slow in com-
prehending the full meaning of Jesus, so were the other
disciples, Nicodemus, and us.

Businessmen, traditionally considered to be the em-
bodiment of conservativeness, are frequently investors
in "get-rich-quick" schemes, such as gold mines, oil,
uranium, or real estate speculation—often losing large
sums of money in the risk for quick gain. Successful
businessmen combine venture with caution. All venture
in business risks a certain amount of failure; but just as
surely, all caution risks no advance or progress. It seems
to me that Philip combined these opposites: He took the
venture of faith in following Jesus; he was cautious about
going all-out on all occasions. For eight years, I was a
member of the Louisiana Baptist Foundation. The
bylaws required that two preachers be members. The
other members were successful businessmen. They had
no hesitancy to risk their *own* money, but they were ul-
traconservative in handling the denomination's money.

When some challenging and far-reaching program is
presented to a church, a Philip is always present, noting
that only x dollars are available. We need those Philips,
practical people who know the value of a dollar, to help

keep us solvent. But we also need some people of faith, such as Andrew, as on that feeding occasion. Philip's calculating mind said:

"There's no way to feed this crowd. We just can't do it with the money we have available."

And we also need an Andrew, saying:

"There is a way; there is a lad here."

Despite Philip's early willingness to follow Jesus, Philip found it difficult to believe and understand everything. For this reason, some scholars have called him a dullard. I can't see Philip this way, for he did have an inquiring mind. In the upper room, at the Last Supper, Philip learned that God is infinitely greater than the mind can comprehend, that God can be seen only through the eyes of faith, and that the best way to know God is to look at Jesus. Jesus had said:

"I am the way, the truth, and the life." (14:6).

Philip was either not listening attentively, or he did not understand what that meant. Many of us, when we don't understand, just sit quietly, trying to bluff it, not wanting to expose ourselves. But not Philip; he said:

"Lord, show us the Father, and we shall be satisfied."

That is a universal longing. We would all like to have something specific and definite to make us certain of God. Other people were always asking Jesus for a "sign." But faith seldom comes that way. So Jesus replied:

"Have I been with you so long, and yet you do not know me, Philip? He who has seen me has seen the Father." (v. 9).

There comes a time when we have to decide on the basis of what we have seen, what we know; we can't always wait for more and more evidence before we decide. This altogether human man did see God in Jesus, and he followed.

One other episode in Philip's life is recorded in John 12:20-23. The scene is what we call the triumphal entry of Jesus into Jerusalem. As usual, there was a great crowd of people. (There's always a crowd of people in old Jerusalem.) Among them were some Greeks who sought out Philip and asked to see Jesus. In this situation, one commentator called him "a guide who could not lead" because, instead of taking them directly to Jesus, he guided them to Andrew. Maybe there was a protocol to follow and Andrew was the "appointments secretary." After all, Jesus was swamped with requests, and someone had to try and protect His time. To me, the important thing is that Philip recognized the opportunity and knew how to meet it.

Many of us need to learn this lesson. If we can't meet a need, get the person to someone who can.

Scripture leaves us without information about Philip after Jesus' death. Tradition tells us that he went to Phrygia with his old friend Nathanael and his devoted sister Mariamne, who became conspicuous in the distribution of food to the needy. Caring for the needy was a mark of the early Christians and is still done by Christians through social service. Later, after the ascension, these three went on to Asia Minor, where Philip became one of the outstanding leaders of the church there. Then he went to Hierapolis, where he was put to death on a cross. After his death, Philip was wrapped in sheets of Syriac paper and papyrus reeds because he felt unworthy to be wrapped in linen as was Jesus.

In AD 195 Polycrates, bishop of Ephesus, writing to Victor, bishop of Rome, stated that

Philip, also one of the twelve apostles, died in Hierapolis, and so did two of his daughters, who had grown old in virginity.

And another of his daughters, after having passed her life under the influence of the Holy Spirit, was buried in Ephesus.

What, then, are we to say about Philip? He was altogether human, shy and retiring. In three of the four incidents recorded of Philip, he was sought out by others: twice by Jesus and once by the Greeks. He was not the outgoing kind of person who sought out others; he stayed more quietly on the sidelines. Although Philip was willing to follow, he took time to make up his mind. When Jesus called him, Philip talked matters over with his friend Nathanael. Facing the hungry crowd, Philip took stock of the situation. When the Greeks came, Philip consulted Andrew. He was not the kind of man who did things on his own initiative.

Traditional, conservative, and cautious to a point but venturesome, dependable, and willing to be open to the new at other points—that's a combination not often found. Once we see it in a person we can know there is something solid.

7

Nathanael
"Still Water Runs Deep"
John 1:43-51

Scholars generally concede that Nathanael and Bartholomew are the same person. Together they are the names for the personal and patronymic name. Nathanael is a Hebrew name meaning "God has given." Bartholomew means "son of Tolmai." Thus we could say, "God has given a son to Tolmai." In the Synoptic Gospels, the name is always Bartholomew and is linked with Philip. In the Fourth Gospel, the name is Nathanael and is also linked with Philip. Since it is accepted that both names are for the same man, I am calling him Nathanael.

Once I was in a motel room at the Orly Airport in Paris, France. I was listening to a British Broadcasting Corporation religious radio program. My notes of the program read:

Bartholomew means "a water divider." Even in our down-to-earth world, we have a sneaky suspicion that there is another world—God's world, and we all want to be a part of it. There is a little touch which leads us to believe there can be more. This is the work of a Bartholomew (Nathanael)—to show us how to bring the two worlds closer together.

Let's use our imagination and enlarge on John 1:43-51. The scene is in the quiet little village of Cana. Nathanael lived there. He was an earnest and sincere Jew

who was looking forward to the coming of the Messiah.
The scene gives us some insight into Nathanael's character and personality. Whenever a devout Jew wished to be
alone and meditate and pray, he would sit under a fig
tree. So that's where Nathanael was when Philip found
him.

We see a man who knew how to be alone. Silence and
quiet didn't bother him. This is a discipline more
preached than practiced. Many of us have the TV, radio,
or stereo—or all three—going all the time. On those rare
occasions when we are alone with ourselves and our
thoughts, we find the solitude so frightening and frus-
trating that we have to get some noise going to preserve
our sanity. Put some of us city dwellers in a rural setting
and we long for the noise of the city. Too many among
us can't stand silence.

I have a Jewish acquaintance whom I've met only
twice. The first time, he was en route to Israel for the first
time. He was not religious, but he wanted to see and feel
the roots from which his people came and to study in
Israel.

Two years later he came by my office for a talk. This
sophisticated New Yorker had been living alone in the
Sinai in a house he had built himself from scraps he
scrounged. Living in solitude, he had had a remarkable
experience with God. His shack had become his "fig
tree" as he meditated on the Law, both "day and night"
(Ps. 1:2). He had not become a Christian, but he had
become a more devout Jew.

Nathanael knew how to live with silence, and he also
had a capacity for great dreams. The world's great
dreamers are those who know how to be alone with
themselves in the quietness. It's hard to dream in the
midst of hectic activity. I should think one of the difficult

features of being president of the United States is in not
having time to be alone to think and dream. People in
every profession need time to think and plan. I know
preachers need that kind of time, and I don't see how
doctors, secretaries, lawyers, teachers, carpenters, or
corporation executives can do without it. But when do
they have the time?

There is no telling how many times Nathanael and
Philip had sat under that same fig tree and shared their
dreams about the Messiah and the restoration of Israel.
That's the feeling one gets in reading John. When Philip
found Nathanael, he had been reading about Jacob, or
that's the impression one gets from the later conversation. Nathanael was reading about Jacob's dream about
a ladder with angels going up and down between heaven
and earth . . . about Jacob wrestling with the angel and
receiving a new name—Israel, which means "one who
prevails with God." At any rate, Nathanael was beginning to wrestle with the idea that this new teacher from
Nazareth he'd been hearing about had some of the characteristics and just might possibly be the Messiah for
whom he and Philip had been waiting.

After meeting Jesus and deciding to follow him, Philip
went to Nathanael and said:

"Nate, I've found him!"

Nathanael thought about Nazareth, that little place up
the road from Cana, as a rather insignificant and uncouth
town. Not Nazareth! Surely the Messiah couldn't come
from a place like that! So he spoke the only sentence
recorded of him:

"Can any good come out of Nazareth?"

This is the one sentence by which he is remembered.
Whoever heard of Plains, Georgia? Can a president of
the United States come from such a place? Yes!

But Philip merely said, "Come and see," and off they went. Jesus saw Nathanael coming and said of him:

"Behold, an Israelite in whom there is no guile!" Nathanael was stunned, and stammered:

"How do you know me?"

"Before Philip called you, when you were under the fig tree, I saw you. I reached out before your friend confirmed your thoughts and prayers. Because of your honest wrestling with your doubts you are a true son of Jacob. Now I promise you greater things. Jacob saw a ladder set up to heaven and 'the angels of God ascending and descending on it.' You will see heaven opened and the angels ascending and descending upon the Son of man. You are looking at Him of whom that ladder is just a picture. You will see and be with Him who is the link between heaven and earth."

Remember that British broadcast I mentioned about the suspicion that there is another world, God's world, and that we want to be a part of it? Well, Nathanael linked his life with Jesus as the fulfillment of his dreams of that world of God.

Dr. Kenneth Shamblin, Methodist bishop of New Orleans, tells of a couple who moved to this country. They did not understand our language very well, but they risked all the money they had on a lottery ticket and won six thousand dollars. When they were paid, they took the money to a bank with great happiness. Then, after much confusion because they could not understand English very well, they were made to understand that they had been paid in counterfeit money. The police were called in. The husband panicked and tried to escape because he was afraid they would think he was involved in the counterfeit crime. The wife finally talked her husband into giving himself up. He discovered that instead of wanting him as an accomplice to the crime, the police simply needed him as a witness against the people who had been carrying on the crooked scheme. The story ends with the couple walking into their shabby apartment, returning to the dull routine of life. The man took his wife's hand in his and said: "Now we must go back to our ten-cent dreams."

Many among us have had it that way, having our great dreams, seeing them shattered, then having to be satisfied to give our minds, time, ability, and life to those things which are insignificant, ten-cent dreams. But not Nathanael! He longed to be a better man, always aspiring and praying. There in his garden, under his fig tree, he found a place where he could be alone with his thoughts and dream great dreams. How he must have longed for their fulfillment.

Then he met Jesus. Nathanael did not long remain a quiet, reserved, and contemplative person. Jesus came into Nathanael's life, and his character was transformed, his personality was revolutionized. Nathanael never got away from his quiet time; he just left the shade and security of his fig tree and became involved with the Man from Nazareth.

Nor do we need to live with ten-cent dreams. We can aspire. We can work. We can achieve. But we do need inspiration and motivation. I submit that we can find what we need in Jesus Christ.

In his book *Twelve Who Were Chosen*, William Barker tells about a man who went on at great length about the questionable weaknesses of Christianity. A wise friend quietly pointed up to some stained-glass windows of a church building. From the outside the windows were grimy and grey-colored with dirt.

"Don't look like much from out here, do they?"

The critic agreed.

"Well, come on with me."

And they went inside the church. There, on the inside, the light was shining through the windows, bringing out all the rich colors and patterns of a figure of Christ. Said the man:

You have to be on the inside to see him. If you stand on the outside and discuss and argue about him forever he will mean little to you. Get on the inside, into the fellowship of the church . . . if you are not already. Get on the inside, into the pages of the Bible, if you have not done so. Get on the inside, into his presence, by getting on your knees and turning yourself over to him. Get on the inside, into an attitude of taking him seriously. Then you will see him as more than just another man. You will find he is the teacher, the Saviour.

Nathanael did that; he got on the inside. No longer looking at grimy, shabby Nazareth and arguing if the Messiah could come from a place like that, he got on the inside with Jesus. And that made a decided difference. It always does!

After the crucifixion, Nathanael was a member of the group that went fishing with Peter at Capernaum, back in the home territory. During that seashore breakfast, those men reaffirmed their faith, renewed their vows, and rededicated their lives. The last time Nathanael is mentioned is with the people in the upper room when a replacement for Judas Iscariot was chosen.

The legendary material about Nathanael (Bartholomew) is varied. Jerome mentions a "Gospel of Bartholomew." There are three separate, but not necessarily contradictory, traditions about Nathanael's ministry.

1. He went with Philip to Phrygia and Hierapolis.
2. He went to India.
3. He was martyred in Armenia.

The Indian account includes this personal description:

> He has black curly hair, white skin, large eyes, straight nose, his
> hair covers his ears, his beard long and grizzled, middle height;
> he wears a white colobium with a purple stripe, and a white
> cloak with four purple "gems" at the corners; for twenty-six
> years he has worn these and they never grow old, his shoes have
> lasted twenty-six years; he prays one hundred times a day and
> one hundred times a night; his voice is like a trumpet; angels
> wait upon him; he is always cheerful and knows all languages.

This is not a very savory description, and we must take
it with some skepticism and make allowances.

There is some early evidence to confirm the Indian
tradition. Said Eusebius:

> Pantaenus . . . advanced as far as India . . . to have found that
> the Gospel according to Matthew had anticipated his own arriv-
> al among some who knew Christ and to whom Bartholomew,
> one of the disciples, had preached and left them the book of
> Matthew in Hebrew script, which is also preserved until this
> time."

From this it would seem that Nathanael (Bartholomew) founded a Christian church in India. In later
years that struggling "mission" church once sent some
messengers as far as Alexandria, Egypt, asking for Christian teachers. They were saying as some of our mission
areas say to us: "Come over and help us."

A fifth-century martyrology refers to the feast day:

> On the ninth Kalends of September the natal day of St. Bar-
> tholomew the Apostle who was beheaded for Christ in Citerior
> India by order of King Astriagis.

An eighth-century martyrology of the Venerable Bede
has this entry:

> The natal day of St. Bartholomew the Apostle who, preaching
> the Gospel of Christ in India, was flayed alive and being be-
> headed by order of King Astriagis completed martyrdom.

And a tenth-century Byzantine tradition says that

> the Apostle Bartholomew went to India *Felix,* or "Happy,"
> which is a translation of the Sanskrit word *Kalyana,* the name of
> a city near Bombay.

Another tradition is that Nathanael was martyred in
Armenia at Albanopolis—modern Derhand—south of
the Caucasus. This has been the claim of the Armenian
Church, which has revered Bartholomew as their founder for some 1,400 years. There is a ninth-century reference to

> The Natal Day of Bartholomew the Apostle who preached in
> Lycaonia . . . in the end was flayed alive by barbarians in Albano
> a city of Major Armenia; and by order of King Astriagis he was
> beheaded and thus buried on the 24th of August.

It is hard to reconcile Nathanael's being killed in both
India and Armenia by the same king. But we can assume
that a king named Astriagis had something to do with his
death.

One of the special days in the Christian calendar,
though of minor importance so far as most are concerned, is August 24, Saint Bartholomew's Day. The occasion marks the anniversary of the "Massacre of Saint
Bartholomew," a tragic event that took place in Paris in
the year 1572 when 30,000 Hugenots (Protestants)
fighting for religious liberty were put to death.

What if you or I were to be remembered for one question we had asked early in our religious journeys? If we were to judge Nathanael by his "Can any good come out of Nazareth?" we would miss his real character and not know the kind of person he became.

Two chapters back I asked you to think of a sentence by which you would like to be remembered and gave you two of mine. Now I'd like to add some others: "Don't take yourself too seriously." And a church member said one of mine should be: "There's another way to do it." Then, my wife adds for me the rabbinic: "On the other hand."

When Nathanael asked his question, Philip acted wisely. Instead of arguing with his friend, Philip merely said, "Come and see." And bless ol' Nate, he didn't argue either; he checked it out for himself. Nathanael found Jesus Christ to be the Savior for whom he was looking. And Nathanael gave his life to that Man from Nazareth.

Some of you may be scornful or skeptical, yet seeking. I invite you to "come and see" for yourself just who this Jesus is. Turn your life over to Him. Get on the inside of the Christian faith and see what a difference it can make.

8

Matthew
"A Man Can Change"
Matthew 9:1-9

Matthew and Levi are obviously the same person. Mark's Gospel says, "Levi the son of Alphaeus" (2:14). So again we have two brothers, the third set, for there was an apostle named James, son of Alphaeus. We do know that Matthew was a tax collector. A fourth-century commentary by the great bishop-scholar, John Chrysostom of Constantinople, shows that there was a strong early tradition that both Matthew and James were tax collectors. Well, that's a new profession added to the predominate fishermen. These brothers were no doubt acquainted with the fishing businessmen. They probably collected the "internal revenue" from them for Rome. Maybe they were the accountants for "Zebedee and Sons." Any business likes to have a good accountant who knows the tax laws, the shelters, and the write-offs.

The actual scriptural information about Matthew is negligible. Not a word of opinion survives within the Gospels. Although very little is known personally, a great deal is known about Matthew's profession; thus we can infer some things about him and the kind of person he was.

Tax collectors were likely to be prosperous and were certain to be regarded with loathing contempt from their fellow Jews for cooperating and collaborating with the occupying power for their own financial gain.

They were particularly despised within the Jewish community as sinners and outside the Law. Matthew's Gospel describes Jesus Himself classing tax collectors with Gentiles and harlots, as the lowest of the low, in His condemnation of certain scribes and Pharisees: "Truly, I say to you, the tax collectors and the harlots go into the kingdom of God before you" (Matt. 21:31). The Jews grouped tax collectors with murderers and robbers, excluding them from testifying in court and excommunicating them from worship in the Temple. In Jesus' parable about the Pharisee and the publican (tax collector), He has the publican "standing afar off" to do his praying, not only because of his own sense of unworthiness but because he had been excommunicated.

Tax collecting was a lucrative business. Rome relieved itself of the expense of collecting taxes in the provinces by putting the franchise up for auction. The highest bidder got the tax concession. Highly skilled employees, usually local people, were hired. Josephus tells of one named Joseph, from the village of Phicola, who established himself at Jerusalem. From there he directed the collection of taxes from Syria, Phoenicia (Lebanon), Judea, and Samaria and held the position for twenty-two years. He had an office in Alexandria from which his steward made payments to the royal treasury. Such men established themselves as bankers and wholesale traders at Jerusalem and mortgaged the land and crops of the peasants.

Suffice it to say, being a tax collector was a lucrative position. It still is—if not financially, at least as a political power base. There's hardly a more powerful position today than that of tax accessor.

Rome had two kinds of taxes: statutory and customs. Statutory taxes included one tenth of the grain crop, one fifth of the wine yield, a 1 percent annual income tax, and a poll tax equivalent of one day's pay per year. These rates were well known, and there was little possibility of abuse.

The customs dues, export and import, were the main source of revenue. The tariff varied from 2.5 percent to 12.5 percent of the value of the goods, about the same as today. There was a sales tax on everything bought and sold. There were also road tolls, bridge tolls, traveler's tax, river crossing, harbor, and quay tolls. You see, we're not so progressive in our taxes.

Matthew was an educated man, perhaps the most learned of the twelve. How else can you explain his business sense and his ability to keep an accurate record of a complicated system? He was at least the equivalent of a modern certified public accountant. And we see his skill later in compiling his Gospel. Matthew was an ambitious man, determined to get rich, to be successful, to be "somebody," no matter what the cost or how the method.

Where did we ever get the idea that the twelve apostles were poor, ignorant peasants? We've made them to appear that way, and I've never fully accepted that. This study of these men has confirmed what I've always believed about them. But perhaps I've looked for data to confirm my idea. Researchers do that, you know. Maybe they were not educated by our standards; nevertheless, they were prosperous businessmen: keen, sharp, and shrewd. They could hold their own with any of us.

Remember, the tax concession went to the highest bidder. All monies collected over and above the authorized levy could be kept by the collector. He could legally collect as much as his ingenuity, resourcefulness, and clout would permit. Rome didn't care, just so long as she got hers. Anything they collected above Rome's levy was pure gravy, lagniappe, and they loved that gravy. They were "riding on the gravy train with biscuit wheels."

To the government, Matthew's job was important. Insofar as taxes were concerned, his word was law. Men obeyed and did what he said. He was a man of authority. Those whose goods passed under his inspection were careful to stay in his good graces. Bribery was a part of the business world twenty centuries before our current businesses and governments came on the scene. No doubt, some expensive spices and silks were passed on, just as an overloaded truck today going through a weighing station drops off a barrel of oysters or a crate of avocados for the man who runs the scales. No doubt, Matthew enjoyed the power and prerequisites of his position.

However, what success Matthew achieved was at great cost to himself. All tax collectors were despised. Rome abhorred them for their corruption and deceit; their high tax levies made Rome look bad. Do you remember the story of Diogenes going through the streets of Athens at midday with a lighted lantern looking for an honest man? Well, a Roman historian named Tacitus once erected a statue *to an honest tax collector.*

The Jews loathed the tax collectors for their collaboration with Rome. To collect taxes from one's own people and then to pay them to alien occupiers was despicable! They sold their souls and their people to gain money. In the process, they lost esteem. No wonder men like Matthew were shunned, unwelcome at social functions, their word no good in court, their money unacceptable in the synagogue. Well, that may be a bit too

strong. I recall a story about the old-time evangelist Billy
Sunday, who was chided for accepting money from a
racetrack gambler. The evangelist squelched his critic by
saying: "The devil has had that money long enough!"

Tax collectors were sinners. No one ever showed any
concern about them and their problems. No one, that is,
until Jesus came along.

In the loneliness of his estrangement, Matthew must
have asked himself a thousand times if he had made a
good bargain. Surely, he must have longed for a way out.
We don't know, but I would say that Matthew's personal
dissatisfaction caused him to turn to the Scriptures. People do that, and Matthew was a Jew, acquainted with the
Scriptures. Unfortunately, it often takes a personal crisis
to get us back to the Bible. Then Matthew heard about
a strange man who had come out of the wilderness, John
the Baptist, they called him. This John was saying:

  "Repent! Prepare the way of the Lord, make his paths
  straight."
Matthew's heart quickened. Yes, he could repent and
change, but how?

Then another man came on the scene, a man from
Nazareth whom they called Jesus. He was saying things
more beautiful than anything Matthew had ever read or
heard. Jesus and His group began to headquarter around
Capernaum. Can't you visualize Matthew, at the edge of
the crowd, listening as Jesus spoke? Matthew's hopeless-
ness recognized some hope.

Matthew's encounter with Jesus took place at Capernaum after Jesus had healed a paralyzed man at Peter's
house. Capernaum was almost in the center of the north
shore of the Sea of Galilee, astride the road from Damas-
cus to the Mediterranean port of Acre. With traffic both
on the road and on the lake, the customs office was in the

center of heavy commerce. Matthew had seen and heard enough to convince him. However unlikely a prospect he may have been, he was ready to make a change. But how? Then one day Jesus stopped at the tax office, looked Matthew in the eye, and spoke to him. Listen to Matthew's own account:

> Getting into a boat he crossed over and came to his own city.
> . . . As Jesus passed on from there, he saw a man called Matthew sitting at the tax office; and he said to him, "Follow me" And he rose and followed him (Matt. 9:1-9).

Just like that! No quibbling, no stalling for time. A straight-from-the-shoulder invitation got an immediate, affirmative answer. Matthew was ready. He had a new experience: Someone believed in him. An entire new life was beginning for a man named Matthew.

Luke 5:29-32 describes what followed. The first thing Matthew did was to have a big dinner (a fish fry?) for his fellow outcasts in his own home. He must have been a man of means to have a house large enough for that. Maybe his brother James was co-host. But why a dinner for his cronies? Well, no one else would have come, for one thing. A better reason is that those were the people who needed Jesus the most. This was a way for Matthew to announce his new faith and declare his changed way of life. His fellow sinners would have a chance to hear this good news for themselves. That's a first impulse of a new Christian: tell someone else.

What happened to Matthew following that dinner party is a mystery. We know that he was a part of Jesus' ministry. Matthew's name is listed in the Book of Acts, indicating that he was loyal through the trial and crucifixion and into the early life of the church. But how did his fellow Capernaumites look at him? Probably with disbelief, some skepticism, and a bit of hesitancy, sort of a wait-and-see attitude.

Have you ever lived in a small town where there were the "town sinners"? Every revival they were on the prayer list. The visiting preacher was asked to visit them; the locals didn't want to. On occasion I've seen such sinners listen and accept Christ as Savior. On occasion I've seen churches and church members shun such converted sinners. But for the most part, I've seen people and churches rejoice, reach out, and welcome such converted sinners. That's all the church is: a bunch of converted sinners. I rather suspect that's what happened with the people of the synagogue in Capernaum; they welcomed Matthew.

The site of Capernaum today is the village of Nahum, standing on a site where a Byzantine church was discovered in 1921. There is a partially restored synagogue— maybe the one attended by Jesus, but probably not. There are the familiar Jewish symbols: The menorah (seven-branched candlestick), the shofar (ram's horn), and the shield of David. There are also some Roman symbols. This could explain the story in Luke 7:1-10 of how a regimental crest of a Roman legionnaire came to adorn a Jewish synagogue.

Subsequent tradition about Matthew is fantastic and contradictory. But there is general agreement that Matthew's ministry began among fellow Jews. His Gospel, written for Jews, bears this out. Thereafter, an infinite variety of opinion exists from Ethiopia, Persia, and Macedonia. Clement of Alexandria said that Matthew died a natural death. The Jewish Talmud gives a rather late account of Matthew's condemnation and death at the hands of the Sanhedrin. Beneath the fantasy of these legends lies a vein of truth: A man died for his faith in a country far from his homeland.

Matthew was a disloyal Jew who had accumulated wealth by shady practices. Before Jesus called him, Matthew was a shrewd, calculating man with no thought of anyone but himself. After accepting Jesus' invitation, Matthew became an other-person-centered man. In Jesus' hands, this man was changed and molded into another form.

This should tell us that the doors of the church should be open to everyone, for there are possibilities in every person.

Paul Quillian tells a story about Sir Phillip Bridges, the organist at Saint Paul's Cathedral in London. Walking in the countryside one afternoon, Bridges came to a village church and asked the sexton if he might play the organ. The sexton looked him over, noticed his cultured speech and dress, and decided it would be all right, so the sexton gave him the key. The sexton stayed in the vestibule. Soon music such as he had never heard came from the skill of the great musician. When Sir Phillip closed the organ and returned the key, the sexton looked at him with awestruck eyes and said: "Sir, I never knew our organ could produce music like that."

Matthew did not know that his life could produce great music. But he found out. When the fingers of the living Christ play on the keyboard of a person's life, heart, and abilities, great music comes out.

"Jesus . . . saw a man called Matthew sitting at the tax office" (9:9). Where others saw a despised person, Jesus saw a man with hidden hungers, divine desires, and a ready heart. The simplicity of the Gospel story conceals the radical nature of what actually happened. Our modern respect for the apostles, for Matthew because of his

Gospel, softens the disrespect the people had for Matthew. We must remind ourselves of those intense feelings.

Further, at the time of Matthew's call, Jesus' movement was beginning to gain momentum and public approval. From the point of view of worldly wisdom, asking someone like a tax collector to accept a prominent place was very unwise. We may not be good at forgiving sinners, but we could tell Jesus a thing or two about good public relations and a good public image. You don't have a sinner in a leadership position. But Jesus knew what He was doing. He knew a man could change.

What kind of an apostle was Matthew? Well, tradition tells us some things. But *read his Gospel:* that was his greatest contribution. Someone said: "When Matthew rose to follow Jesus the only things he took with him were his pen and ink." It is well for us that he put them to such good use. Would that we would change and use our abilities as well.

9

Thomas
"Sure, I Doubted"
John 20:24-29

There are people who postpone a decision about Christ and Christian faith because they feel incapable of living up to it. Not Thomas! Sure, he doubted and was skeptical. But Thomas did not sit around and wait for all the questions to be answered before he started. When Jesus called, Thomas responded affirmatively, without all the evidence and not knowing for sure how capable he was of living up to the demands.

Thomas was a loyal, practical, down-to-earth, seeing-is-believing kind of man. His name is included in each listing of the twelve. The Fourth Gospel refers to him as Thomas "called Didymus" (KJV). Didymus is not a surname; it is a Greek translation of the Hebrew *Thomas,* and both mean "Twin." There has been much interesting speculation about who he was "twin to." Some say Thomas had a twin sister, Lydia. Others say he was the twin of another disciple. The most farfetched comes from the Edessan Christians, who were a strong Syriac Christian community about the middle of the first century. The Edessans rejected the virgin birth of Christ. They said Thomas was the twin brother of Jesus. That is so "far out" that it gained no credence, not even in early days. Thomas was a twin of someone, but we don't know who.

Tradition says that Thomas was a carpenter and stone mason. In the Thorwaldsen Museum in Copenhagen, Denmark, Thomas is depicted in stone with a finger to his mouth, as though in serious thought, and a carpenter's square under his arm. Things had to "square up" for this man.

Thomas was probably a strong, robust, muscular, and hardheaded man. Certainly he was a dynamic disciple, the kind of person with whom modern humans can identify. We can identify with Thomas because he struggled with the problems of belief, doubt, and faith. Pascal wrote:

> There are two classes of men who can be called reasonable, those who serve God with their hearts because they know Him, or those who seek for Him with their whole heart because they know Him not. I have nothing but compassion for all who sincerely lament their doubt, who look upon it as the worst of evils, and spare no pain to escape from it.

Thomas struggled to believe. Thomas's was an honest quest for truth.

The Fourth Gospel mentions four occasions when the presence of Thomas was significant to the story. From these incidents the character of the man emerges with some clarity and force.

First, in John 11, Jesus had been hounded out of Jerusalem and had sought safety in a small village. News of the illness of his good friend Lazarus arrived. Jesus decided to go back to Bethany, within two miles of Jerusalem. This seemed to be a rash decision. Thomas was frightened. He knew the danger, but he volunteered to go along, saying bluntly and realistically:

"Let us also go along, that we may die with him." Thomas, the realist, was also a man of loyalty and cour-

age. He had signed up with Jesus; if following Jesus
meant death, Thomas was ready to go. No fair-weather
recruit, Thomas; he was a voluntary enlistee for the duration.

Second, during the Last Supper (John 14:3-5), Jesus
was saying:
"When I go and prepare a place for you, I will come
again, that where I am you may be also."
Thomas interrupted,
"Look, we do not even know *where* you are going; how
can we know the way?"

It was not that the others understood or knew any
more than Thomas. He was not the sort to let a statement like that slip by. If Thomas didn't understand, he
asked for clarification. Any teacher knows that not everyone in a class understands everything, but most won't
admit it; they sit there looking knowledgeable. But usually there is an "asking" Thomas. We Christians should be
grateful for Thomas's question. Thomas was not the
kind who lives patiently with his questions without ex-
pressing them. Jesus' answer, "I am the way, and the
truth, and the life," was not very specific. Instead of an
effort to convince, it was more of a call to personal loyalty
and trust:
"Just trust me, Tom, I know what I'm doing."
To a practical man, this kind of trust is hard to come by.

The third occasion was in that same upper room after
the resurrection (John 20:25). Thomas had not been
present at any of the appearances of Jesus. When told,
he was skeptical. Who wouldn't be skeptical! I would,
and so would you.
"Unless I see in his hands the print of the nails, and
place my finger in the marks of the nails, and place my
hand in his side, I will not believe."

It is unfortunate that this one sentence has given him the name "Doubting Thomas" and made that a term of approbation—especially in light of his earlier service.

Finally, a week later, the disciples were again in the upper room (John 20:27). This time Jesus was present. Thomas's doubts and demands provided the opportunity that was needed to bring home and nail down the reality of the resurrection. Jesus called Thomas over and said:

"Tom, put your finger here, and see my hands; and put out your hand, and place it in my side; do not be faithless, but believing.

That was enough. Thomas's doubts disappeared as he said:

"My Lord and my God!"

Jesus never scolded Thomas for doubting. Jesus knew that doubt is the father of discovery, just as necessity is the mother of invention. To one who says, "I've never doubted, not for a minute," I say, "Good for you, but how sad; you've never known the joy of struggle or the thrill of hammering out your faith on a tough anvil." Jesus respected Thomas's honest quest for truth.

Never did the other disciples say:

"Tom, you're through! You're a skeptic, a heretic. You can't stay in the church; there's no place for a man like you. We can't have you wrecking the faith of other people."

That kind of thing has happened, and still happens in the church. There are those today who would have no place for Thomas because he does not dot the same *I's* and cross the same *T's* of biblical inspiration that they do. The Lord knows that the Christian usefulness of many has been shunted aside by those who would force them

into a mold. Jesus did not do that with Thomas; nor does
He do it to us.

The disciples loved Thomas. They believed in him.
They respected Thomas's struggle to believe. They
knew there was a place for him. After all, Jesus had chosen Thomas, hadn't He!

The gratitude of the Christian church for Thomas's
wanting to see for himself is recorded in *The Book of
Common Prayer:*

The Collect for Saint Thomas Day, December 21:

Almighty and everliving God, who, for the greater confirmation
of faith, didst suffer thy holy Apostle Thomas to be doubtful in
thy Son's resurrection; Grant us so perfectly, and without all
doubt, to believe in thy Son Jesus Christ, that our faith in thy
sight may never be reproved. Hear us, O Lord, through this
same Jesus Christ, to whom, with thee, and the Holy Ghost, be
all honour and glory, now and forever more. Amen.

Thomas is described by a Greek poet named Eutycus:

Seeing is believing
Was his motto. Better,
Feeling is believing.
The scientific mind requires
Substantial evidence,
Controlled experiments,
With photographs and measurements.
And Thomas was no poet.
Nor would he credit women—
Or even ten apostles.
He required the touch
Of his ten fingers.

Thomas's later years are clouded in mystery. Tradition sends him to Parthyia and India, especially India.

There are three traditions about three places in India: the Punjab, near Madras, and in Kerala. In India the congregation of Saint Thomas claims him as their founder. No other apostle has a church which he founded that is still alive.

Generally speaking, *faith* is the great word we use in church. But I want to say a good word for *doubt*. In our churches, we need to have a healthy respect for doubt. And in some, I believe that we do. No one ought ever to be hesitant about voicing one's doubts. I just do not believe some things. I'm not quite sure of some things. And I'm firmly convinced of other things. On the whole, people are more interested in what we do believe than in what we're unsure about. And, on the whole, that has been my procedure in my ministry: to give an account of affirmations of the Christian faith. I've called them the "Affirmations of a Skeptical Believer," and I feel no hesitancy in sharing doubts with you.

Every one of us has uncertainties, hesitancies, and doubts. Reverent as we are, respectfully as we may listen, earnestly as we may pray, convinced though we may be, every one of us here must honestly say what a man once said to Jesus: "Lord, I believe; help my unbelief." And we can do that in church for two reasons:

1. Like Thomas, we do believe in Jesus Christ, even with some uncertainties;
2. Like Thomas, we are supported by fellow believers who say there is a place for us in church.

Concerning this common problem faced by Thomas and us, let me give two observations.

First, doubt is one of the noblest powers we have. Look at the world today and see the innumerable beliefs and practices from Communism and subcultures to violence and disorder which must be doubted. Some things

I just cannot accept. The great benefactors of society have been those who are distinguished by the fact that in the midst of universally accepted ideas they dared to stand up and shout, *"I doubt that!"* Without the capacity to doubt, there could be no progress, only docile, unquestioning acceptance of the status quo—things as they are.

Second, the strongest faith has always come out of a struggle. The sturdiest faith of biblical persons and other Christians has come out of the struggle with unbelief and doubt. How does faith overcome doubt? It never does—*completely.* But let's emphasize one central experience in all strong believers: They honestly went through their disbeliefs until they began to doubt their doubts. What I am getting at is not for us to stop doubting, but for us to shift our attention and emphasis until we will doubt our doubts and disbelieve our unbelief.

But, you say, that may be all right for some areas, but when it comes to religion, we want faith! Faith in God, faith in Christ, faith in the Bible—of course, we want that kind of faith. We can't get along without it. But anyone who thinks that one can have faith without exercising one's doubts is oversimplifying and will one day run headlong into trouble.

Ah, when we sing the praise of great men of faith, let us remember our indebtedness to those brave doubters who, when false ideas dominated the minds of men and spoiled their lives, saved the day with their courageous doubt.

As you read this portrait of Thomas, you may be struggling with some doubts about God. Well, that's all right. So do I. There are many ideas about God that ought to be doubted. The Bible itself discards one idea of God after the other because men dared to doubt wrong concepts about God. But when it comes to surrendering *all* belief about God to become an out-and-out atheist, have you carried that to its logical conclusion? Take a glance at where that leads: *No God!* Nothing ultimately creative, nothing behind our universe—Can you believe that? Can you *really* believe that? Why, that is incredible!

You who question God, are you willing to carry your doubts to their logical conclusions? Are the products of atheism what you want? Can you take your atheism straight? Are you willing to live by those conclusions? If not, then you'd better begin doubting your doubts and find a way to God.

For many people, faith in Christ is hard to accept. "How can you expect me to believe all that miracle stuff in a scientific age?" But look: Is what really stands in the way of faith in Christ the strain on our credulity, *or is it the demands on our moral character*?

It is not so much—Can I believe certain miraculous events happened to or were done by a man twenty centuries ago?—as it is: Can I believe that certain moral miracles can happen to and be done by me, and am I willing to see if it can happen to me, *now*?

How vividly some of us remember Sunday, December 7, 1941. That was the day the Japanese bombed Pearl Harbor. But we've seen a miraculous aftermath. The pilot who led that attack was Captain Mitsuo Fuchida. Within ten years after that bombing, Captain Fuchida was in the United States training for the Christian ministry so he could return to Japan to proclaim the Christian faith. Incredible? So one would think. Dr. Hiroshi Kondo, once a member of a church I pastored, was a teenaged Kamakazi pilot in that war. Now he is a Christian with a doctor's degree from the New Orleans Baptist Theological Seminary and a respected Christian leader.

How come? Fuchida and Kondo doubted some things and found something else in Jesus Christ. Miraculous? Yes, but miracles still happen.

This kind of thing could happen to you as you read and reflect. You think you can't be transformed by the renewing of your mind by Jesus Christ? In God's name, doubt that doubt, and try it for yourself.

Ah, Thomas, how grateful we are for a man like you! Courageous enough to voice your questions and loyal enough to follow even when you weren't altogether sure. We need to know about you now, for some of us know how it is to be like you.

10

James
"Unknown Celebrity"
Acts 1:12-14

No passion thumps more firmly in more human breasts than the desire to be somebody, to be some kind of a celebrity. We love to fantasize about seeing our names splashed across the front page in big headlines or hearing our name mentioned on national television. We dream about getting off a plane at Kennedy International and having the crowd point at us, saying: "Yep, that's him!" There's some Walter Mitty in every one of us.

Alfred Adler, one of the founding fathers of modern psychiatry, says that the wish to be significant is the dominate impulse of human nature, even stronger than the sex drive, which Sigmund Freud put first.

J. Wallace Hamilton calls this "the drum major instinct." I can identify with that. When I played in the high school band, I yearned to be the drum major. That was in the days before twirlers and dancers. Ours was a military-type band drilled in marching precision. How I wanted to wear the "Shako"—that's the big tall hat with the plume of feathers. Although I'm 5' 10" tall, that was too short. Nick Moore, about 6' 2", who could have strutted with the Olympia brass band, was chosen. One day we were scheduled for a parade down Broadway and Main Street in Oklahoma City. "Squire" Russell, our director, called me over and said:

"Avery, you're drum major today."

Just like that! Man, I tell you there was sheer joy, elation, stage fright, and butterflies in the stomach all mixed up. That was the crowning achievement to climax years of dedicated band service. I was going to be the drum major!

That's an instinct common to us all. When the sales manager says, "Good volume this month, Mac," or a teammate says, "Great tackle, Joe," there is the same elation over being recognized. A friend of mine, Dick Smith of New York, has been in theatrical makeup for forty years. He has a room full of awards: Tonys, Emmys, and Oscars. He received another Oscar for the makeup for the award-winning film *Amadeus*. I wrote to congratulate Dick. He called to say thanks. Then he said the greatest joy is to be appreciated by his peers.

The presence of this instinct explains why most of us are taken in by advertising. Those gentlemen of gentle persuasion know how to take advantage of our consuming desire to feel important. Here's a letter that is typical:

> As you undoubtedly know, your name is on several mailing lists in which you are classified as "highly literate, progressive, interested in world affairs, good literature, and science." Therefore, I know you will be interested in what I have to say.

Interested? I'll say so! Those who can describe me that accurately surely do have my interest, and soon they may have my money as well. But I've learned. These *Who's Who* things come in all the time, even from England. I once had an invitation to join one for "outstanding black personalities." I should have taken that one just for the fun. But there is always a catch in the bottom line: to be included one has to buy the book at a "special prepublication" price of $65.95. My ego isn't that big!

Fame, as such, is one of the most overrated, delusive factors of human existence. In the recognition it bestows on its favorites, it is completely devoid of any sense of proportion. The player who knocks in the most home runs during a baseball career draws more applause, and money, than the scientist who saves thousands of lives in the discovery of a disease cure. (By the way, do you know who Babe Ruth was? Well, do you know the name of the man who discovered penicillin? Sir Alexander Fleming did so in 1928, the year after Ruth set the single season home run record.)

In our house is a trophy case for two boys: one an athlete, the other a musician. The biggest athletic trophy is about three feet high and silver, and there's a gold medallion for a national victory. The largest nonathletic trophy is about three inches high, made out of some nondescript metal. One boy went to college on his legs and the other on his lungs.

The thing is, most of us are not famous; most of us are life's unknown celebrities. The man we're looking at in this chapter is an unknown celebrity. He is the most obscure apostle. Nowhere in Scripture is mentioned anything he said or did. We know absolutely nothing about this man except his name: James, son of Alphaeus. But that is something. I think I'd settle for that where Jesus is concerned.

James, son of Alphaeus, may have been a cousin of Jesus, for his mother seems to have been spoken of as the sister of Mary, the mother of Jesus. If this is true, then this James was also a cousin of James and John, the sons of Zebedee. This James may have been Matthew's brother. He is also known as "James the Less." Maybe this was because he was the younger brother, or he had less ability or was less prominent; more likely it was because he was short of stature.

James obviously came from a good family background. He probably was in the tax-collecting business with his brother, so we can infer some of the same things about him that we did about Matthew. If the conjecture is true that James and Matthew were cousins of Jesus, this might explain some of Jesus' concern for tax collectors and their willingness to follow Jesus.

Something must have prompted Jesus to include James, but we don't know what it was. During Jesus' life and after His death, James lived and died and passed from the scene. He was a background disciple. He is representative of thousands of Jesus' followers, most in fact, of whom there is no record, known for one generation in a small circle, then forgotten. His distinguishing feature is obscurity, and James seems to have been content.

Legend and tradition offer us little more than does the Scripture. The only legend about James says that he went on a mission to Persia, where he was crucified. Yet he epitomizes all those quiet, unassuming, obscure people whose unheralded and unknown contributions have been the backbone of progress.

Most of us are ordinary people, having no exceptional ability. Yet our limitations should not make us indifferent to living life to the best and fullest wherever we are. Our faithful service may go unnoticed and unremembered. But remember this:

> His eye is on the sparrow,
> And I know he watches me.

A tourist was visiting a great cathedral. With much enthusiasm, the guide described the beautiful cathedral, especially two great towers, the beauty of their architecture, the exquisite details of the workmanship. Then he added quietly: "No one knows who built them." What a descriptive sentence! It describes so many: missionaries who do not have an offering named for them, Sunday School teachers who valiantly worked with unruly children, yours and mine, and with us as well. Ah, those "unknown celebrities"! Think of those people in your own life, whom "the world will little note nor long remember," who are celebrities.

"Unknown celebrities" in my life include Merrill Scott, whose father was a Pentecostal preacher. Merrill was the first person who ever spoke to me about Christ; this occurred when I was about twelve years old. Floyd Kimes, "Squire Russell," the high school band director (who let me wear the Shako), and church organist on Sundays, teacher of English literature, created in me the love of and taste for good music and good literature. Ruth Turner, wife of my pastor, spent time with an adolescent, encouraging him to sing, even transposing the music to a lower key so his voice could reach the notes. And others, so many others. As the writer of Hebrews 11:32 put it: "Time would fail me to tell of . . ."

One obscure man that Louisianans should never forget, but already have (other than an educational building named for him in Ruston, Louisiana, while I was pastor there), is John T. Walters. Brother John was eccentric. (That made two of us.) Brilliant mind but little common sense, we said. He never quite "made it" by the world's standards. In the early days, Brother John preached wherever he found a person to listen. He was a prototype of Coleridge's "Ancient Mariner." Brother John rode horses. When they went out of style, he rode the bus as far as it would go; then he would walk the rest of the way.

He planted the seed of the gospel in the remote places of Louisiana. People heard about Christ from those seed and still do. More than one seed matured, but one prominent one is Dr. Carl Conrad, from the Louisiana French country, who recently retired as the director of State Missions.

Who knows, one of us may be a "celebrity" like John Walters. One of you math teachers may have an Einstein.

One of you English teachers may have a Pulitzer Prize winner.

One of your children may be a Leontyne Price.

One of you Sunday School teachers may have another Truett or Fosdick or Graham.

One day, we may be the kind of footnote that Austin Gallaher was—remembered only because he touched someone's life. Who was Austin Gallaher? As an eleven-year-old lad he was swimming with an eight-year-old friend who was seized with cramps and was drowning. Somehow, Austin got his little friend to shore. No one knows Austin Gallaher except as a footnote in history because the lad Gallaher saved was Abraham Lincoln.

You see, someone is always needed for the obscure tasks. Followers are needed as much as leaders.

A great artist once painted the Last Supper and invited some friends to see it. After gazing at it for a while, one of them said: "How beautiful you've painted those cups on the table, such exquisite detail." Whereupon the artist took his brush and painted out the cups, saying: "I want men to look at Christ; He is important here."

One time a Methodist bishop was examining some candidates for ordination to the ministry. He asked them if they had a strong desire for preeminence in the ministry. To a man they replied in meek humility, probably perjuring themselves, that such was not their desire. Said the bishop: "Then, you are a sorry lot!" After the shock had worn off, the bishop explained: "Just be sure it is true greatness you seek."

One time Jesus had said to two apostles who were asking for high appointments:

"No man can give you greatness; you must earn it."

So, back to the "drum major instinct" which to some extent we all possess. Ann Greenwood wrote a verse about a woman who wanted to write a book:

> "Tain't that I wanted money or fame
>   when I'm dead,
> But because I get so tired of compos-
>   ing bread.
> I'd like the folks in Plainville to
>   read some magazine
> An' see it writ in printin', "A Poem by
>   Sarah Green."
> Yes, I can cook, but mercy, a body's
>   got to cook.
> That's the very reason I want to write
>   a book.

Thomas Gray was musing in a church yard. Later he wrote some thoughts about humble and heroic and faithful people who die unnoticed:

> Perhaps in this neglected spot is laid
> Some heart once pregnant with celestial fire;
> . . . .
> Full many a gem of purest ray serene,
>   The dark unfathom'd caves of ocean bear;
> Full many a flower is born to blush unseen,
>   And wastes its sweetness on the desert air.

That's the way some people, good people, live out their lives on earth, their gracious lives unnoticed by the world, the sweetness of their spirit seemingly wasted. Maybe so among us, but not to God. The unknown names are written in and well known in the books of heaven. And the name of James the Less, son of Alphaeus, is there.

There is a greatness that is within the grasp of us all. We are important. God made us that way. Christianity teaches that our personalities are sacred, and our souls have eternal value. Let us, therefore, do as this obscure man named James did and dedicate ourselves to Christ, who came to show us what life can be. Let us outdo ourselves in kindness and service, whether we achieve prominence or not. How? Through a repentant faith that accepts Jesus Christ as Savior and then follows Him in finding that abundant life here and now that He talked about and said could be ours.

11

Simon
"Comes the Revolution!"
Acts 1:12-14

In *King Henry VIII,* Shakespeare describes a disappointed servant of the king by having him say:

> Had I but served my God with half the zeal
> I served my king, he would not in mine age
> Have left me naked to mine enemies.

Our man Simon would not have said that, for he served both the civil cause and his God with equal zeal.

There were two apostles named Simon: Simon Peter and Simon the Zealot. The latter was as obscure as the former was prominent. Except for the listing of Simon's name as one of the twelve, we know nothing about him. However, we can make some reasonable assumptions about his personality and the kind of man he was.

Simon is listed by Luke-Acts in the tenth place and is called "the Zealot," a term which may apply to his own temperament or to his political party or to both. In Matthew and Mark, Simon is number eleven and is called "the Cananaean," which is Aramaic for "the zealous one." That name is not connected with the region of Canaan. More likely the term *kananaios* is derived from the Hebrew word "kant," which means "to be jealous for the law." The exact equivalent for *"kana"* in Greek is *zelotes,* the term used by Luke as "the Zealot." Therefore, the implication is that this Simon was a member of the Zealot party.

In modern terms, we would call the Zealots "terrorists." They were not a gentlemanly group who played by the rules. They were rough, tough, and mean.

From the Maccabean times in the first and second centuries before Christ to the fall of Masada in AD 73, the term *Zealot* was applied to those Jews who were driven by a fanatical and nationalistic messianism. They considered themselves to be the agents of God to deliver their nation from foreign oppression. There is nothing more fierce than someone who believes he is an avenging agent of God. During the Protestant Reformation someone said: "I'd rather face a legion of soldiers than one Calvinist convinced he is doing the will of God."

Those Zealots operated under a creed that said, "No rule but the Law: no king but God!" They became increasingly violent in their resistance both to the Roman occupation forces and to their own fellow Jews who collaborated with Rome or who adapted to Greek culture and customs.

The emotional climate and the people of Galilee, from whence came eleven of the apostles, was fertile soil for discontent and revolt. There is a New Testament report of some Galilaeans "whose blood Pilate had mingled with their sacrifices" (Luke 13:1). This could have been one of those times when Rome squelched an uprising.

This party of fanatical nationalists was progressively taken over by extremists who resorted more and more to terrorism. Such men banded together into a group called the Assassins, or Sicarii, after the word *sica*—a small dagger which they concealed under their robes. This group attracted all kinds of men of violence, sworn to achieve their ends by the assassination of both Romans and their fellow countrymen who they thought had compromised with Rome. Josephus had little good to say of them:

> Zealots, for that was the name these reckless persons went by, as if they were Zealous in good practices, and were rather extravagent and reckless in the worst actions.

The world still has its terrorists, everywhere.

A typical Jewish patriot, such as Simon detested all that Rome stood for. In this respect, he was like many citizens of the nations of the world who have been under a foreign power. Listen to one of them:

> Is life so dear or peace so sweet as to be purchased at the price of chains and slavery? Forbid it, Almighty God! I know not what course others may take, but as for me, give me liberty, or give me death!

Our American forefather Patrick Henry said that. Why, today we'd put Pat Henry in jail if he said that.

In the past two decades, we have seen many under-privileged nations gain political freedom, and there will be more. Though many nations are smaller than Louisiana, they are full members of the United Nations with one full vote, the same as the United States has. Some of their words, as well as some of their deeds, are fiery, revolutionary, bellicose, and somewhat contemptuous.

That was the kind of dream Simon the Zealot had. He wanted his people free. He wanted Israel restored to its rightful place. With Simon's dreams we could agree, but we might quarrel with his method.

The Zealots had a worthy cause which they felt justified their bitterness and violence. Most of the Jews had become resigned to their fate, learning to live the best they could under undesirable circumstances. A few had started to work for the Romans as tax collectors and other civil servants. But not these renegade vigilantes! They would as easily thrust their "sica" into the back of a Jewish friend of Rome as into the belly of a Roman. They talked a good deal about brotherhood, but along the way they dropped the brother and kept the hood.

Those Zealots left a tragic picture and accomplished very little. Their fires left Jewish homes in ashes, but Rome was unhurt by the flames. That's the way it was here in the 1960s during the "burn, baby, burn" riots; those who were supposed to be helped were the ones most hurt. We see the same thing happening in today's South Africa.

Such was the background of Simon. There may have been two other apostles much like him, Thaddaeus and Judas Iscariot. It is downright astounding, if not incredible, that such a man could associate with a man like Matthew, shoving aside disparate loyalties in a common loyalty to Jesus, to keep faith with Him through His crucifixion and resurrection, to be present at Pentecost, and to carry His message of love to the Gentile world. Beyond Pentecost, there is no biblical mention of Simon.

We don't know why or how Simon came under Jesus' influence. There is no account of any personal meeting, no description of His call. Maybe Simon heard Jesus speak; certainly, Simon heard about Jesus. Perhaps Simon saw some changes, even in a man like Matthew. He could have felt at first that this Jesus was the answer to his prayers for a leader who would restore Israel. The great miracle is that Jesus chose Simon at all. To choose a member of a seething underground movement, a violent revolutionary, would seem unlikely. Rome's spies would know about Simon and thus keep a closer watch on Jesus' group to see if they were also revolutionaries. But Simon isn't the only one whose choice *we* would question: What about some of the others? However, there was a work Simon could do. This is another example of Jesus' all-embracing love, all-encompassing intention, and all-purpose use of all kinds of people.

Fire out of control in a forest or a skyscraper or a home is a devastating, destroying thing. The wild unmanageable fire burning in the hearts of people can be equally destructive. But fire under control is beneficial: It gives warmth, cooks food, and runs industry. Nothing is more relaxing or gives greater contentment than to be with people one loves around an open fire. So to control a firebrand personality and give it a constructive method for its cause is a beautiful thing. Jesus did that for Simon. Oh, Simon still longed for his people to be free from Rome. But his passionate zeal took on a new dimension. Simon still blazed, but he was under control.

For three years Simon lived with Jesus. He grew in mind, heart, and spirit. No doubt, Simon preached about Jesus with zeal—a pulpit pounder. This is a reasonable assumption because his name appears in every list before the crucifixion and after the resurrection. Tradition says that Simon remained loyal till his own death, preaching in Africa, Persia, and eventually in an island country we now call the British Isles.

Does Simon's life-style contain any message for us? Yes, very definitely, for Simon gives us hope. If Jesus could use a man like Simon, with his reputation, surely there is a place for us. And if Simon and Matthew could get along together in the same group, putting aside their personal differences, today's church members can do no less.

Take forgiveness, for example. Among the twelve was a man named Matthew, one of those Jews who had "sold out" his people for personal gain by collecting taxes for hated Rome. Matthew was the kind of man whom the Zealots despised and sometimes killed. The interest, concerns, and life-styles of these two men were widely divergent and contradictory. Now they found themselves in the same group. Maybe they were suspicious of each other, saying:

"What's a man like him doing here? Better keep an eye on him."

Perhaps there were arguments, even fights. But Jesus had called both of them. The miracle of forgiveness affected them both. They learned to respect each other, to understand a little of why each had done as he had; more, they learned to trust and love each other. They had begun to work in a common cause. Commitment to Jesus Christ is so powerful that, when we live in it, reconciliation is possible. That is, *if each wants to be reconciled.*

There is another lesson for us. Although we need the quiet passive types—and must have them—the world is changed by the zealots, the enthusiasts. At the turn of the last century, the Marquis of Landsdowne became distressed about the low moral tone of the town of Colne. He wrote to the vicar of the village church to ask what steps could be taken to improve the conditions. The vicar wrote back:

"Send us an enthusiast!"

When Simon joined the twelve, that's what he was, an enthusiast; he brought in some zeal.

By nature I am not a zealot, at least not like Simon. Nor am I a Casper Milquetoast. I'm sort of in between, with a leaning toward Simon. While I know what it is to stick one's neck out, and have done so on numerous occasions for something in which I believe, I couldn't become a member of the Sicarii—never that for me. I would look on myself as more of a "quiet revolutionist" than as an active guerilla.

Trailblazers are needed to go into the uncharted places to cut the path and mark the way. Others are needed to come along and clear out and begin the development. Then others are needed to consolidate the gains and give stability, plus to keep alive some of those earlier dreams to encourage others to go out and blaze new trails.

Where would we be without some of those zealous revolutionists? Martin Luther or John Calvin, for example. Where would America be today had we not had some revolutionists in 1776: Adams, Franklin, Jefferson, Madison, and Washington?

Where would women be today were it not for yesterday's Susan B. Anthony, who was once jailed because she broke the law by voting in an election?

Where would modern nursing be had there not been Florence Nightingale?

Where would civil rights be today were it not for Martin Luther King, Jr., or Caesar Chavez?

I do not condone the violent methods of the Igrun or El Fatah or the IRA or even the Calvinists. But because we would not always do what we knew to be right, some militant crusader had to use spectacular methods to get our attention and cause us to get moving in those right directions.

In choosing Simon the Zealot, Jesus let us know that no type of personality is excluded; by having Simon and Matthew together, we learn that opposites can serve together.

12

Judas
"May I Ask a Question?"
John 14:22-27

One legend says that a little boy named Jude was with the shepherds at Bethlehem. He was too young to tend the sheep, so he was kept busy doing little errands. There is always a place for errand boys in a group of men. Boys like to be with men. That's why they will shag balls at practice or gather up the equipment. Such boys are needed, both for the thankless tasks they do and the fact that men like to have children around. It's good for boys to be around men.

One night a strange thing happened in the hills around Bethlehem. Strange sights and heavenly voices filled the night. Finally, one of the shepherds said:
"Let us go over to Bethlehem and see this thing that has happened."
And little Jude tagged along. They found a mother and a newborn baby. When the others returned to the sheep, Jude stayed. Seeing the look of wonder in Jude's eyes, the kind of look any child has while standing around the crib of a new baby, Mary smiled and gently placed the infant in Jude's arms so he could "hold the baby," something every child wants to do.

Thirty years passed, and this lad named Jude was selected for the "cabinet" of the baby he had once held in his little arms, for that baby was now a man, Jesus of

Nazareth. That's a tender, touching story with a lot of human interest in it. But that's all it is—a legend. But it has a great dramatic touch; so let's pretend that it may have happened that way, just for the human touch.

There is some problem of identification of the apostle listed number ten in Matthew and Mark and called Thaddaeus, and listed number eleven by Luke and called Judas, son of James. The name "Lebbaeus" is also used in some texts. Both Thaddaeus and Lebbaeus mean the same thing: "bighearted or large chested." So Judas may have been a burly, barrel-chested kind of man. He was probably a tenor; barrel-chested men usually are, for such a chest gives a good resonance chamber, and the thick neck has the proper vocal chords. Judas's voice would have carried well in an open-air crowd. Judas was probably an outgoing, gregarious personality. His earlier experiences with the shepherds had taught him how to get along with people. And he was probably still doing errands for people.

If we are to limit the apostles to the same twelve men, a simple process of identification makes Judas, son of James, and Thaddaeus-Lebbaeus the same person. This also helps distinguish him from the other Judas.

The name *Judas* was an honorable name which went back to the founder of the tribe of Judah. It gained prominence by its association with Judas Maccabeus, the great leader who had gained Israel's independence from Syria. But the name is no longer honorable, for it is too closely associated with the man who betrayed Jesus.

There is some documentary evidence, mostly tradition based on legend, that Judas (Thaddaeus-Lebbaeus) was also a member of the Zealot political party. In two of the oldest manuscripts called the "Apostolic Constitution," concerning the administration and structure of the early church, Judas is described as

"Thaddaeus, also called Lebbaeus, who was surnamed Judas the Zealot."

If this be the case, it could explain the only words Judas spoke that are recorded in the New Testament. Judas asked,

> "Lord, how is it that you will manifest yourself to us, and not to the world?" Jesus answered him, "If a man loves me, he will keep my word, and my Father will love him, and we will come to him and make our home with him. He who does not love me does not keep my words; and the word which you hear is not mine but the Father's who sent me.
>
> "These things I have spoken to you, while I am still with you. But the Counselor, the Holy Spirit, whom the Father will send in my name, he will teach you all things, and bring to your remembrance all that I have said to you. Peace I leave with you; my peace I give to you; not as the world gives do I give to you" (John 14:22-27).

The setting was the upper room; the occasion was the Last Supper. There was an impending sense of doom, of final tragedy; their cause seemed to have been lost. Judas the Zealot couldn't understand why it had to be that way. He had been associated with a "lost cause" before, and he knew how that felt. But Judas had thought the cause of Jesus was the real thing, sure of success. He seems to have been saying:

Lord, it's not us whom You need to convince. We believe that You are the Messiah; it's the rest of the people who need convincing. Isn't it time You took charge of things, time for You to show who you are, to show Your power?"

Jesus seems to have replied in the same tone and mood as He had at the temptation:

"Thad, you can't win people's love by a display of force their loyalty, maybe, but not their love. Force is a strange thing. Let a stronger force come along, and people will switch their loyalty. Only when a person gives his heart, his love, himself, will my Father and I really possess that person so that that person will know inner peace."

Then, as if in direct contradiction to the Zealot principles:

"Thad, My greatest wish for you is peace, not violence. But it's My own kind of peace, the kind of peace you cannot achieve or acquire by worldly methods. This kind of peace comes from the inside."

From Jesus' answer to Judas's one question, there are three conditions to following Jesus:

1. We must have and know Jesus' commandments. And we do. We can be thankful that we have a written record of what they are: love one another as God loves us, and preach the gospel as God's witnesses.

2. We must love Jesus; and if we love Him, we will keep His commandments.

3. We must do what He tells us to do.

All of this is vital today. There are those to whom Jesus is reality, even with a touch of love and devotion, but their loyalty and service is suspect.

After Pentecost, the Bible records nothing more about Judas (Thaddaeus-Lebbaeus). There is plenty of fascinating legendary material, however. There is a document called "The Acts of Thaddaeus," and there is a letter said to have been written to Jesus by Prince Abgar of Edessa. Abgar was ill and wrote to Jesus asking him to visit and to heal Him. Abgar also said that he had heard of the plots to kill Jesus and offered Him sanctuary and safety in Edessa.

Jesus declined, saying that He had been sent to Israel alone. But Jesus promised that after His ascension He would send one of the disciples to cure the king and preach the gospel.

Judas (Thaddaeus-Lebbaeus) was the one who was sent. He healed the king, and he preached. Edessa, now named Urfa in Turkey (or Uria), was in Persian Mesopotamia. This legend is popular in the Eastern churches and goes back to the close of the second century; it is found in Eusebius's *Ecclesiastical History*. When Abgar commissioned him to preach, Judas (Thaddaeus-Lebbaeus) replied:

> I will preach in their presence, and sow among them the word of God, concerning the coming of Jesus, how he was born; and concerning his mission, for what purpose he was sent by the Father; and concerning the power of his works, and the mysteries he proclaimed in the world, and by what power he did these things; and concerning his new preaching, and his abasement and humiliation, and how he humbled himself, and died and debased his divinity and was crucified, and descended into Hades, and burst the bars which from eternity had not been broken, and raised the dead; for he descended alone and rose with many, and thus ascended to his Father.

This reply is a remarkable summary of the Christian creed and preaching of the early Christian missionaries.

Since this man bore the same name as the one who betrayed Jesus, Judas lost some esteem among the early Christians. So we have an early example of "guilt by association," a practice which still goes on. Many innocent people suffer because of guilt by association. Why do we continue to allow this to happen?

This Judas finally "lived down" some of the under-served guilt. The Christians who believed in prayer to the saints never invoked this name except when all the other saints had been appealed to in vain. It was a sort of "We've tried everyone else and failed, we might as well try ol' Jude; we've nothing to lose." Thus, by "popular veneration," this Judas has become the patron saint of the desperate and despairing.

For Roman Catholics, Saint Jude's Day is October 28, while the Eastern Orthodox Church observes June 19. Now Jude has become the patron saint of healing. Entertainer Danny Thomas may be partly responsible for this, for Thomas has put a lot of time and energy into raising millions of dollars for the Saint Jude Hospital in Memphis, Tennessee. This is a hospital dedicated to the most desperate medical problems of children. The combination of excellent medical ability and prayer has resulted in some miraculous achievements. At this hospital, no child is turned away.

In the middle of the third century, Christian leaders, such as Origin and Tertullian, said that the Epistle of Jude was written by this apostle. Today most New Testament scholars disagree. I would like to believe that this delightful, pungent little work did come from this man. Such a hearty, robust man could have written it. The picturesque language of a poetic soul is there; some choice humor is to be found, and it would take a strong man to write such sharp criticism. The writer must have known Jesus quite well. The Epistle of Jude is as relevant as any New Testament writing. Yes, I would like to think that our man wrote it, but the evidence is too weak; so we can't even lift Judas out of obscurity with this epistle.

The title of this chapter, "May I Ask a Question?" helps me identify with this man. I've always been a question asker. My questions are not usually asked audibly. I never was one to question in class. Most of the questions were on the inside, and I quietly went about seeking answers for myself: reading, thinking, praying, or in personal conversation with a professor or friend. And I've found a lot of answers for myself, answers which I share with others as they seek answers. Some questions cannot be answered in words; the answers are found in an experience, in an emotion, or in a mood. For example, "Do you love me? How much do you love me?" Neither a lover nor a parent can fully answer such questions. Oh, an affirmative answer can be given. But unless love is actually present as something that can be felt, the words don't really answer. The feeling, the experience, the mood satisfies.

Jesus didn't really answer Thad's question in so many words; instead, Jesus pointed him to a feeling and a task.

My now-deceased friend Blake Smith, longtime pastor of the University Baptist Church in Austin, Texas, said that he once had a dream: He had died and gone to heaven. This surprised Smith's enemies and even some of his friends. In the dream Smith said:

"Lord, may I ask You a question?"

"Of course, son."

"Is it true what they say about You on earth?"

"No, son, but they mean well."

I still have some unanswered questions to which I'm still seeking answers. Those questions don't really bother me, certainly not enough to keep me from believing and following Jesus Christ. Why, I already know more than I need. And I'm certain that these other things will fall in place once I get the feeling and have the experi-

ence. I'm convinced about Jesus Christ; that's enough
for now. And I've found much of the inner peace about
which Jesus told Thaddaeus that night.

To those of you who ask questions about Jesus and
Christian faith, I say:
"That's all right; keep on asking, for that's the way you
learn."
Maybe some of you don't need to ask questions because
your faith is all you need. That's all right too. You see,
we are different kinds of personalities and the same attitude and approach doesn't work for everyone. Let us not
discourage the honest seeker by disparaging his ques-
tioning attitude. To all of us I would say:
"We know enough about Jesus Christ to make a decision about him. There are many areas of life where we
don't know everything, but that doesn't keep us from
acting. I don't understand electricity, or TV, or phar-
macology, but I trust them and make decisions to use
them for their benefit. No scientist understands everything about his own field of study, but he does act
upon what he does know in order to learn more. I'm
sure enough about Jesus Christ to believe in him, accept him, and commit my life to him because I've seen
enough positive evidence and experienced a lot of
confirmation. I recommend this Jesus to you and urge
you to let him become a part of your life."

13

Judas Iscariot
"He Was Numbered Among Us"
Acts 1:15-17

Judas Iscariot is one of the most controversially complex and interesting characters in the New Testament. He has fascinated writers, dramatists, theologians, and preachers ever since he appeared on the stage of history. He has been analyzed and discussed from almost every possible point of view. Some have been totally condemnatory. Some have tried to be understanding and explanatory. But most have been puzzled.

The New Testament refers to Judas Iscariot nine times, but we know surprisingly little about him. What we do know is enough to start heated discussions, even arguments. The Gospel writers themselves, as we would expect, were in agreement as to the dastardly nature of Judas's deed of betrayal. We would expect them to point out the heinous quality of that act. Nevertheless, the Gospel writers appear to be almost as puzzled as we are.

The story of Judas Iscariot, more than any other member of the twelve, has gathered accretions and interpretations. The character and motive of this man have been under constant analysis. We watch Judas in a kind of mesmerized fascination of horror and pity: horror for the deed and pity for the man. *Why did he do it?* All four Gospels refer to him as Judas Iscariot, and all four use the qualifying epithet about betrayal.

Who was this man, and what do we know about him? What little there is in the New Testament is mostly derogatory. Legend and tradition have little to say that is constructive, and there is no effort to understand the man and his deed. Anyway, Judas had nothing to do with the early traditions because he had committed suicide. But maybe we can get a little bit of insight by looking at what little we do have.

Look at the name *Iscariot,* for example. *Iscariot* might have been an adaptation of the Aramaic word for a dagger-man. The Latin *sicarius* and the Greek *sicarios* are each derived from the word *sicarii* (dagger-men)—as we saw in our discussion about Simon. So the implication is that Judas was a member of such a group.

Another theory coming from a word study links *Iscariot* with the Greek word *scortia* and the Syrian word *scariot,* which means a leather jacket. This jacket had purselike pockets which would be useful for an itinerant treasurer, which Judas was.

A more likely meaning of *Iscariot* comes from the Hebrew language: *Ish* means "man of" and *Kerioth* was a village in the hills of Judea. This would make Judas "the man of Kerioth," the only outsider in the group since all of the others were from Galilee. As a Judean, Judas may have been of a more dispassionate, calculating bent than the emotional and impassioned Galileans.

From all this, the composite would be a man who was a member of a group of terrorists, an outsider, essentially a loner, lonely, never really accepted, and feeling misunderstood.

Even so, Judas Iscariot was chosen by Jesus, and he accepted the call. We say that Jesus was a clear reader of personality and a good judge of character. Jesus chose Judas and even appointed him treasurer of the apostles.

That shows Judas could be trusted with an important office. But why wasn't Matthew, the man accustomed to dealing with money, made treasurer? Jesus must have seen in Judas a potentially useful member of His team, and Judas must have seen in Jesus the potential fulfillment of the messianic prophecy.

Matthew and Mark did not seem interested in Judas's motives, only in the fact of his betrayal. In the incident of Jesus' annointing by Mary of Bethany (John 12:5-6), John implied a motive of greed. Judas did ask on that occasion whether the money Mary spent on the ointment could not have been better spent on the poor. But to be accused of greed or theft just does not fit Judas's character or Jesus' confidence in him. There was little to have been gained financially by joining this itinerant group. The incident seems to reflect some retrospective thinking by John.

John was harder on Judas than any of the other Gospel writers. Listen to some of the things John called him: thief, betrayer, possessed by the devil, son of perdition— as if he could not paint Judas black enough. After all, other apostles had at one time or other betrayed or misunderstood Jesus.

When Luke said, "Satan entered into Judas" (Luke 22:3), we can understand that. There are those sudden volcanic fires in human nature which do erupt, leaving destruction. There are those lionlike temptations which spring upon our virtue and overcome us before our resistance can begin. And there may have been jealousy or proud ambition or disillusion in Judas to prompt that demonic spirit. There was also ambition in James and John, and on occasion Peter seemed jealous of the closeness of John with Jesus.

Two ideas may give us some insights into the man known as Judas Iscariot.

For one thing, recognizing that which is on the inside threatening the whole of our lives is hard. Maybe this is what Luke meant in saying, "Satan entered into Judas."

How often we could understand the actions of people, perhaps even help them, if we just knew what was going on inside them. Let's put it another way—if we just knew what was going on inside ourselves! Hopes and fears, frustrations and defeats, anxieties and concerns, joys and sorrows, dreams and aspirations are going on inside us that sometimes even we do not know about until something happens to jar us. That's when we need someone, perhaps a trained counselor, to help us take a look, understand, and learn to live with the mixture of emotions and motives that we all have.

This is one thing that happened to Judas. Whatever was going on within him was unknown to the other apostles, and perhaps even to himself. What if Jesus had taken Judas aside for a quiet talk, as He had taken that "inner three"? Maybe He did; we don't know. What would Jesus have said to Judas if they had met later and Judas had repented instead of committing suicide? I believe Jesus would have been gentle and forgiving. There would have been another, different embrace and kiss.

The second idea is: A temptation has no power unless it is directed toward some weakness. We may even be unaware of the weakness.

We are coming more and more to realize that the temptation to the excessive use of alcohol, for example, comes from some weakness, either physical or emotional. I think the same thing is true of the drug culture, where, perhaps, peer approval is the weakness. Other weaknesses can be seen when a person goes on a sex binge or a gambling splurge or indulges in character assassination through gossip. There is a weakness, else there would be no temptation. And it is no disgrace to be tempted: *We all are!* The problem comes when we yield. There was some weakness in the character of Judas. When the temptation came, he succumbed.

I do not understand the character of Judas; nor have I ever found an analysis of him that fully satisfies me. Why did Jesus choose a man like Judas to be one of the twelve men who were to carry out His mission? Was Jesus capable of making a wrong choice? Did that choice mean that Judas began on an equal basis with the others? Were the apostles "saved" men upon their being chosen by Jesus?

This poses an interesting dilemma. When Jesus called the twelve, they responded affirmatively, including Judas. And I believe Judas was on an equal basis with the other apostles. Jesus must have seen the same possibilities in Judas that He saw in the others. He would not have selected Him otherwise.

If Judas were "predestined" to betray Jesus, meaning Judas had no choice, we would be too harsh in blaming a man for doing something over which he had no control. It would be a peculiar God who would "predestine" a man to such a fate and then condemn him for eternity for fulfilling his destiny. That violates every concept of God that I have, everything I believe the Bible teaches us about God. *Judas did not have to betray; he chose to betray.*

Of crucial importance in any person's life is the inner response to the events which life brings. One's destiny is tied to the responses one makes to life experiences. I believe Judas made his own decision. He was responsible for that decision. He participated in everything. He heard Jesus speak and saw what He did. Judas had a choice, just as the others, just as we can choose. And Judas made his choice. After all, the other apostles failed Jesus too. Peter publicly denied that he knew Jesus, and that was in a matter of minutes after Judas's betrayal. The only one to stay with Jesus throughout the crucifixion was John; the others scattered.

Where do we fit into this picture? Well, in many places. But there is an all-too-significant sentence about Judas in Acts 1:17 which can fit too many of us: "He was numbered among us." That is, Judas was a name on the apostles' roll. And that is a chief liability of the church in our day: names on a roll but not a part of the enterprise, in an outward relationship but not inwardly a part of it.

In an article written before the death of the League of Nations and before the birth of the United Nations, Albert Einstein inadvertently gave a picture of this attitude. Explaining his feeling about the League of Nations, he said: "I am rarely enthusiastic about what the League of Nations has done or not done, but I am thankful that it exists." That frank expression of a tepid, nonparticipating approval serves up with deadly exactness the attitdue of many in the church who are merely numbered among the company—just names on a roll, rarely enthusiastic but grateful that the church exists.

There is another way this liability manifests itself. Judas was an unfulfilled possibility. Weymouth translates this verse in Acts: "Judas was reckoned as one of our number, and a share in this ministry was allotted to him." That is, Judas staked out his claim, but he never worked it. His possibilities didn't pan out. Disraeli once described some of the elder statesmen of his day as being "extinct volcanoes." Once there was fire, heat, and light, but no longer.

Much of the impotence of today's church comes from

those who stake out claims and leave them unworked. The greatest danger to the church does not lie in a godless communism or an atheistic materialism or a secular humanism but in our failure to give a visible demonstration of working our allotted area. That was not the purpose of the twelve; nor is it the purpose of today's church. Those apostles changed their community by turning it upside down, all but Judas Iscariot. So should we. God forgive us when we initiate nothing.

Obviously, Judas misinterpreted Jesus and His cause. But, James, John, and Peter also misinterpreted. Judas did turn sour on the whole thing. Whatever got into him—Satan, those volcanic fires—he betrayed. Judas even repented when he tried to give back the money. But his repentance led in the wrong direction: *He committed suicide!* Mere repentance is not enough. Repentance can sometimes be mistaken for remorse for an evil deed or a sense of guilt for having done wrong or frustration at having been found out. True repentance is a complete turning around, a change of purpose, a new direction for life.

As we look at Peter, we can see the same thing happening in his life that happened to Judas. The difference is in Peter's repentance. For Peter, repentance meant a change in his life. Peter must have asked:

"Can Jesus ever forgive me? Does he care for me? Does he love me, too?"

Peter took the opportunity to find out. In the TV film *Jesus of Nazareth,* there is a scene toward the end, just after the resurrection, where Peter is speaking to the disciples in the upper room:

"I betrayed him. We all betrayed him. But I feel forgiven."

Then the camera zooms in for a close-up of Peter's face, and, looking directly at the viewer, Peter says:

"We are *all* forgiven."

Unfortunately, Judas didn't take that opportunity. If he had, he would have found and experienced that same love and forgiveness.

So, what about us? Well, there is a touch of Judas in us, just as there is something of the other apostles in us. We have heard Jesus' call, and most of us have answered affirmatively. We have had our times of betrayal, mostly minor but sometimes major. We have been numbered among while not always fully being a part of Jesus' cause. We have had a ministry allotted to us. We have possibilities that are still untapped.

What do we do now? *We decide!* We make a choice, for which we are responsible. We can truly repent and know the forgiving love of Jesus Christ, and in that experience we can find new purpose and new direction for our lives.

14

Matthias

"Getting into the Game Late"
Acts 1:21-26

Venice is one of the most beautiful cities of the world, not only for its physical beauty but more for the unique character of the city and its magnificent art and architecture. One of the exquisite places is the Doges Palace. In the council chamber is a frieze of the figures famous in the history of Venice. In this series of remarkable portraits running around the wall, there is a noticeable gap, as if one of the pictures had been removed. In this empty space is a black tablet with this inscription: "This is the place of Mariono Falieri beheaded for his crimes." That blank space in the cornice of this Venetian "Hall of Fame" marks the disgrace of a man. The epitaph records the national detestation of a man's dishonor.

This striking memorial to the disloyal Doge illustrates the omission of a name from the portrait gallery of the twelve which Luke gives in Acts 1:13, where only eleven names are given in his list of the original twelve apostles.

The 11 apostles and 120 other disciples had gathered again in that upper room following Jesus' ascension. Peter called upon them to fill the place left by Judas Iscariot. The replacement was to be someone who had been associated with them from the beginning, from the time of John the Baptist till that moment. Another qualification was to have been a witness to the resurrection.

The real test was not what was known about Jesus, but to have really known Him.

Two names were proposed: Joseph, called Barsabbas, who was surnamed Justus; and Matthias. After earnest prayer the vote was taken, and Matthias was selected. Tradition says that both men were among the seventy Jesus sent out two by two during His early ministry. Neither man is mentioned elsewhere in the New Testament. However, most of the others aren't mentioned either.

In the apocryphal literature, Clement of Alexandria, in the late second century, says that Matthias, like Matthew, had been a tax collector. Clement also says that both men were vegetarians. Now where would he find a tidbit like that? A sixth-century story originating in Egypt relates that at the partition of the world among the apostles, the land of the cannibals (man-eaters) fell to Matthias. That is irony if he were a vegetarian.

There are several lessons we can learn from the selection of Matthias.

First, even in religion, there is routine, the necessity for organization and structure. In the sixties, especially, we saw a lot of rebellion against organization, against institutions. Many young people rebelled against "the institutional church." I don't like a lot of structure, either, but we must have some. Organization can become a straitjacket in which the Spirit is paralyzed, but Spirit without any framework whatsoever can be like wind with no sail to catch it. A jellyfish is the least structured of all creatures, but who wants to be like that?

Years ago a development was begun which was called "the church within the church," that is, small groups who rebelled, saying, "The institutional church is dead." But immediately they set up a structure which was even more rigid than that from which they came. Even the "Jesus People" did that. Much as we say we dislike it, there must be some framework, some plan of organization. Those apostles and disciples saw this. They realized that there was a need to fill the vacancy caused by Judas's defection; so they called a business meeting.

Second, vacancies in the structure do occur. Vacancies are not always created by default. Sometimes people do drop out, maybe not so dramatically as did Judas, but they may go sour, get their feelings hurt, get themselves out on a limb that is cut off, or whatever. But sometimes a vacancy occurs by death, disability, transfer, or even by getting changed to another position. It is tragic to have a vacancy caused by a vagrant Dodge or a disloyal Judas. However, vacancies, whatever the cause, do not kill an organization. None of us is indispensable. Someone is selected to replace.

Third, note that Peter took the lead. Maybe he had been chosen, or perhaps the force of his personality led the way. At any rate, someone needed to take the lead, and Peter did. Even in a group of "leaders," someone must preside.

Fourth, Matthias accepted the responsibility, even if he had not been one of the first chosen. He did not pout or refuse because he was a replacement or a substitute.

In athletics, everyone wants to be a "starter," a member of the first team. Repeatedly we hear the phrase, "Play me or trade me." I can understand that, but there is a need for the substitute with ability, someone who comes off the bench, gets in the game late, and delivers by making something happen.

Quarterback Earl Morrall was like that. First with the Baltimore Colts and then with the Miami Dolphins, he played in the shadow of Johnny Unitas and Bob Griese.

But twice, when the stars were injured, Earl Morrall took those teams to the play-offs by coming off the bench, getting into the game late.

One of my favorite stories is about the Texas Aggies. No, not one of "those" jokes. In the early years of football, before it got so organized, the squads were small. In one game, the Aggies had so many injuries that there were no more substitutes on the bench. The coach sent up into the stands to get a player from the student body. That caught on as a tradition, so today the Aggie student body stands throughout the game, "just in case" the coach has to call on one of them. That never happens, of course, but it does symbolize a readiness.

What relevance does Matthias have for us?

Well, a church always has some gaps or vacancies which need to be filled. No matter what the cause, we need replacements. There is some place, some task for everyone.

Being obscure in church is no new thing. Most of us are obscure, some because we want it that way. There are plenty of obscure people in the Bible, but they did have a part in the story. There is no more obscure person in the Bible than Adam and Eve's other son, Seth. To Adam and Eve, Seth awakened hope. With Abel dead and Cain a fugitive, how would God's promise of future generations be fulfilled? In a word, the future lay with Seth. Despite the fame of a few, the future is always with Seth —the ordinary person who, in unspectacular ways, becomes extraordinary. That's the way it was with the twelve chosen by Jesus. Most of them were obscure, but without them where would Jesus' message of "good news" be?

There are two insights I'd like us to see.

First, we must trust our own slice of life. It's rather

easy to identify with Matthias or Seth. There is a little bit of Cain in me, for there has been some temper and anger but never enough to kill anyone. There have been a few flashes of Abel's goodness, though, heaven knows, not the devout goodness that arouses anyone's jealousy. No, I'm more like Adam's other son—rather ordinary in matters of both evil and goodness. Let's face it, most of us are destined to be ordinary people—Adam's other child; the one selected by lot.

And there's nothing wrong with that!

Matthias came on the scene, was asked to take a job, took it, did it, and then died. And that's the way it is for most of us so far as worldly note is concerned. When we die, most of us will be listed without comment. The question is whether this fact will make us permanently discontented, frustrated with our lot, and envious of others; or will it lead us to trust our slice of life, enjoy it, and do with it what we can?

The second insight is that ordinary people are important in the ways of God.

Matthias's obscurity is a reminder of that importance: He provided continuity. He was a carrier of the "good news," without whom the spark would have gone out. After the desertion of Judas, someone had to take his place.

As for the early church, glimpse at the record, as Paul put it in the sixteenth chapter of Romans, and see how many you know: Andronicus, Ampliatus, Urbanus, Stachys, Aristobulus, Herodion, Narcissus, Tryphaena, Tryphosa, and eleven others. Such folk comprised the church of Paul's day. They were all Matthiases.

Sure, we like to have heroes—outstanding people. We need them. But who and where are they? Time was when we could name them, even without the media. Ours seems to be an "age of Matthias." So to paraphrase Lincoln: "God must have loved the Matthiases of the world; He made so many of them."

Who are the Matthiases in your congregation? And in the hundreds of thousands of churches across the world? They pay their bills on time and stay out of trouble with the law. Their lives pass like the most regular of verbs—punctual at work, home each evening, except when they bowl or fish, interested in family, and unfashionably loyal to their spouses. They are the neighbors next door who mind their own business but whose smiles are friendly. They are the ones who aren't swept away by politicians but who always vote. The Matthiases don't understand "selling short" or "capital gains," don't read *The Wall Street Journal* but try to put some money in the bank and give to the church. They would be lost in a gourmet French restaurant, but their families get excited over a bucket of fried chicken and a picnic in the park. Their clothes are undistinguished and their travels as few; but when the hat is passed for a sick friend, they have a few bucks to spare.

Matthias is the ordinary person.

Matthiases' demands on life are modest, but their joys and sorrows run deep. They are the stuff on which the order of the world rests. When Matthiases pass from the scene, few will notice, fewer will remember, and even fewer will celebrate the homegoing of the beloved pilgrims. But when they enter the church triumphant, it will be to the fanfare of trumpets, the singing of the heavenly hosts, and an outstretched hand and a voice saying: "Welcome home! Well done."

There is a line from Shakespeare's *King Lear* which fits: "That which ordinary men are fit for, I am qualified in and the best of me is diligence."

We have looked at the apostles, all thirteen of them. We have seen that some portion of them is in each of us. We are like them.

None of the thirteen fully understood Jesus. Each saw something in Jesus that appealed to him. They believed in Jesus. They saw God in Him. They accepted Him as the Messiah. Each of them brought a distinct personality to the gospel enterprise. Then each discovered that he could not mold Jesus into his concepts. Rather, the apostles had to conform to Jesus' mold.

You see, this Jesus of Nazareth cannot be put into a box, neatly labeled, and filed. His work is not completed. He still walks the earth, saying: "Follow me!" And we respond—celebrity or obscure—we can respond and follow Him. There is a place for us in "the glorious company." Whatever our idiosyncrasies, abilities, or limitation, *there is a place for us!*

Lord, bless us with a sense of worth
   However brief our stay,
     However slightly known,
       However faint the mark we make.
Let it warm our hearts to know that
   we are children of Thy hand,
     And children of Thy grace and love.
      Through Jesus Christ our Lord. Amen.

        —Martin Luther Harvey, Jr.